Landscape Archaeology and Ecology Special Series

Papers from the Landscape Conservation Forum

Volume (1) Dynamic Landscape Restoration Art or Science?

Ian D. Rotherham and Christine Handley (eds.)

August 2012

Edited by Ian D. Rotherham and Christine Handley

ISBN 978-1-904098-37-9

Published by:
Wildtrack Publishing, Venture House,
103 Arundel Street, Sheffield S1 2NT

Typeset and processed by Christine Handley

Supported by:
Biodiversity and Landscape History Research Institute.
Sheffield Hallam University.
HEC Associates Ltd.

© *Wildtrack Publishing and the individual authors*

All rights reserved. No part of this publication may be reproduced or transmitted in any form or by any means, electronic or mechanical, including photocopying, recording, or any information storage or retrieval system, without permission in writing from the publisher.

Landscape Archaeology and Ecology Special Series - **Papers from the Landscape Conservation Forum: Dynamic Landscape Restoration, August 2012**

CONTENTS

INTRODUCTION	1
OVERVIEW AND ISSUES: THE ETHICS OF CONSERVATION AND RESTORATION CHOICES, OPTIONS AND TRADE-OFFS *Penny Anderson*	3
SUSTAINABLE DEVELOPMENT AND GREEN NETWORKS IN URBAN AND POST-INDUSTRIAL LANDSCAPES *John Box*	10
LANDSCAPE LANDFORM SIMULATION: PEAK DISTRICT TRIALS *John Gunn*	19
STOWE: THE CONSERVATION OF A DESIGNED LANDSCAPE *Richard Wheeler*	21
WILDLIFE AND COAL - THE NATURE CONSERVATION VALUE OF POST-MINING SITES IN SOUTH YORKSHIRE *Ian D. Rotherham, Jeff Lunn and Frank Spode*	30

Landscape Archaeology and Ecology Special Series - **Papers from the Landscape Conservation Forum: Dynamic Landscape Restoration, August 2012**

DYNAMIC LANDSCAPE RESTORATION:
Art or Science? - Introduction

Organised by **The Landscape Conservation Forum**, this event was aimed at all those involved in the conservation and restoration of sites and landscapes, be they degraded post-industrial environments, damaged historic parklands, urban greenspace or agricultural areas. Speakers and participants included landscape professionals, archaeologists, ecologists, earth scientists, planners, conservationists and those in education.

The day was intended to challenge current thinking and raise questions relating to restoration or reclamation; 'habitat' creation and conservation; and the philosophies and ethics which underpin the various approaches. As always, the Forum hoped to raise the broader issues and to promote the debate between and across the various professional and academic groups.

Programme

Introduction and welcome: Dr Ian D. Rotherham Sheffield Hallam University and Chair of the Landscape Conservation Forum.

Morning Session Chair: Ken Smith Peak National Park Authority.

Professor Carys Swanwick, (University of Sheffield): *Setting the scene*.

Jeff Lunn, (English Nature), Dr Ian D. Rotherham and Dr Frank Spode (Sheffield Hallam University): *Wildlife and Coal: the nature conservation value of post-coaling sites in South Yorkshire*.

Dr John Box, (Wardell Armstrong, Environmental Consultant): *Sustainable development and green networks in urban and post-industrial landscapes*.

Professor John Gunn, (University of Huddersfield): *Limestone Landform Simulation: Peak District Trials*.

Afternoon Session: Chair: Dr Frank Spode, Sheffield Hallam University.

Richard Wheeler, (National Trust): *Stowe: the conservation of a designed landscape*.

Ken Smith and Rhodri Thomas, (Peak National Park Authority): *Ditching the Dirt on Dirtlow Rake: a case study in industrial restoration*.

Kate Clark, (English Heritage): *Conservation Plans - a common language or a crutch?*

Penny Anderson, (Penny Anderson Associates, Ecological Consultant): *Overview and Issues: the ethics of conservation restoration*.

Concluding remarks: Dr Ian D. Rotherham, Chair, Landscape Conservation Forum.

OVERVIEW AND ISSUES: THE ETHICS OF CONSERVATION AND RESTORATION CHOICES, OPTIONS AND TRADE-OFFS

Penny Anderson
Penny Anderson Associates.

INTRODUCTION

Archaeology, historic landscapes and ecology have much in common, as is evident from the preceding papers. This presentation attempted to draw out these common themes, examine some of the rationale behind them and, finally, provide some thoughts on the conference title "*Dynamic Landscape Restoration: Art or Science*".

Many of the papers addressed restoration, conservation and creation or re-creation. It is important to be mindful both of what we mean by these terms, and that others often interpret them differently. Restoration more closely signifies repair or renewal. Historic buildings are restored to their former glory; habitats are repaired after damage, such as the moorlands here in the Peak District after fire or trampling damage (Anderson *et al.*, 1997). The key to a restoration project is that there is a relict or semblance of the previous feature which can be treated.

Creation or re-creation is more properly reserved for new projects starting from something else (as when a new woodland or pond is created in grassland or in an arable field) or from nothing – a new building on a new site. For the archaeologist, creation or re-creation are reserved for reconstructions, out of context, usually in an educational or interpretational setting to aid understanding. The ecologist might similarly be reconstructing an image of a particular habitat.

Conservation surely is more to do with protecting the feature of value and preventing it from deterioration by suitable management. This might equally apply to managing a habitat to prevent it drying out, being encroached by scrub, or becoming rank, to a species population (say tigers), to a geological exposure or to an historic monument. All these are conserved *in situ* and in context. Some historical artefacts are, of course, conserved in museums and collections rather than *in situ*, but these suffer from a loss of historic context. Protecting species in zoos or gardens have similar implications.

This historic context is extremely important for habitats, geological and geomorphological features, archaeological and historic sites. All these features developed at a particular time and place in a particular physical climate, through management, and under the socio-economic conditions of their period. This applies equally to ancient woodlands, the kinds of new industrial wildlife landscapes described today, and to all historic features of whatever age. They are a function, often, of a particular combination of processes which were themselves related to natural and anthropological factors. They are essentially a product of their history and have taken time to develop. This historic context is a feature which tends not to be sufficiently valued by ecologists.

ISSUES IN RESTORATION

Turning back to restoration and creation or reconstruction, we are constantly faced with a range of dilemmas exemplified by the Stowe case study. How do we decide what to restore? A garden just as a habitat is constantly evolving as new plants, new ideas or financial constraints play their part. Similarly, a habitat now, or 100 years ago, exists in an entirely different context to one 500 years ago. The surrounding seed sources and pressures from wild animals differ, management had different functions and requirements which we can often only guess, the climate and pollution load were different.

Deciding what to create or restore therefore involves making value judgements. They depend on our understanding of the historic situation, on the quality of what remains, the extent of character still preserved from some past period, the money available to restore particular features, but also a degree of fashion. There are vogues, for example, for creating ponds and ox-eye daisy grassland, but marshes, bogs and flood meadows are less favoured. This is partly related to images – flowery meadows "caught on". There are horticultural versions in gardens, flower patches in parks, new meadows in

Figure 1. Restoration of damaged ground surrounded by existing habitat in the moorlands of the Peak District.

landscape schemes. The seed is commercially available, and some relatively cheap. Flowery meadows have had a good press – Prince Charles has one, they win prizes at the Chelsea Flower Show, anyone can grow one – at least according to the media and the seed advertisements. Ponds, similarly, are popular, children like them, and anyone can build one that will function adequately. The key to this appeal is science. Enough research has been conducted on species, methods, seed production, collecting, cleaning and storage, and appropriate machines have been developed to enable wildflower meadows to be established relatively easily. New research is now allowing us to think about the restoration of lead rakes, and limestone dale morphology, as described by other speakers.

Deciding what to create or restore thus also depends greatly on our knowledge base and on the availability of the necessary materials and machines. But there is more to the decision than this. We also need to decide on our template. Are we trying to restore an eighteenth century garden, a seventeenth century house, an ancient wood or a 20-year old meadow? Do we lose the eighteenth and nineteenth century additions in order to reveal and restore the splendours of the older house or garden hidden behind them?

The decision in ecological terms will be dictated by the extent of vestiges of the desired state, and the ease with which this can be restored. In Europe, it is often culturally derived habitats which are being created or restored. Our meadows, pastures and heaths, for example, are essentially man-made communities developed from the original wildwood, or colonising naturally after disturbance. Over time, they have acquired specially adapted plants and animals which we now value highly, and which are threatened by the huge scale of habitat loss. Not having any original habitats left unaffected by human activities makes attempts at their re-creation difficult without a local template.

THE NORTH AMERICAN EXPERIENCE

It is interesting to compare this approach with that in America where habitat restoration is of considerable interest. The original concept was of restoration to the original, pre-European, vegetation. Hence, restoration was used in the way habitat creation is defined earlier – to re-establish what would once have been the natural vegetation. Two particularly interesting events arose out of this approach. First, by collecting seed from vestiges of prairie grassland alongside rail tracks and observing how, where and whether it grew in various restoration projects, it was discovered that some species were typical of a prairie fringe or savannah type community which had previously not been known to exist (Jordan & Packard, 1989).

Secondly, as the restoration projects began to mature, it was realised that, far from being natural, many of America's vegetation types were bound to the management the various Indian tribes had exerted on them.

There is, of course, a fundamental deficiency in even attempting to re-create or restore any past splendour, particularly of habitats. The modern replica is without any meaningful evolutionary context. The factor of time intertwined with history is not available. The genetics of the plants will be different, the management, machines, functions and purposes which dictated the evolution and development of the old one won't be the same and, most importantly, the soils, their nutrients, horizons and animals will have little in common with old ones.

Several important points follow from this. First, the conservation *in situ* of long-established features of interest is of paramount importance. In some cases, it may also be necessary to maintain the context and links to such features so that their historic evolution is also visible and interpretable. The protection and integration of the coaltip heaths and other habitats into the Green Network in Telford is a good example. Secondly, it is clear that if a site is translocated, it is the site context, meaning and history which are always lost, let alone any deficiencies resulting from the translocation process itself.

The arguments presented so far lead to the conclusion that habitat creation cannot replace the value of the long-established sites (and this does not just mean the ancient ones, but also some of the best industrial landscapes as well), whereas successful restoration is possible from a feature which is not badly degraded, and where all the elements survive as relics on the site or can re-invade from surrounding areas (including invertebrates, fungi, and bryophytes, for example).

The importance of habitat creation lies more with direct ecological benefits for plants and animals and with potentially huge nature conservation opportunities that engage the public and stimulate an interest in the natural environment. The ecological potential lies with helping the more common and mobile species to spread and expand their populations with connecting isolated habitats back together, and by providing buffers to sensitive areas. For the public, successful habitat creation can look good, be attractive and pleasant to be in, provide stimulation, colour, smells and a "wildness" previously equally lacking in a highly productive agricultural landscape or an urban environment.

SUCCESS

The key to such benefits is "successful". How do we ensure that habitat creation is successful? This is where I believe the best practitioners are practising the art of applying science tempered by experience and value judgements. Habitat creation is certainly not just based on science. We do not know enough for that. Let me give you some examples. Most habitat creation takes place on soils previously used for some non-ecological land use – farming, buildings, forestry, and so on. The soils are generally far from pristine, and generally hold levels of available nutrients well above those found in long-established or species-rich habitats (Gilbert & Anderson, 1988). Yet most practitioners have species richness as an objective for their new habitat. We do not have the scientific information to know properly which species will not out-compete its neighbour in a particular soil type, climate and nutrient levels. Decisions have to be based on personal experience of communities and ecosystems elsewhere, on the kind of information collated in the *Biological Flora of the British Isles* (published in the *Journal of Ecology*), of research and monitoring of others' trials and experiments, of the autecological data such as that gathered by Grime and his colleagues (e.g. Grime *et al.*, 1988). Based on such information, species lists are selected, and relative abundances in the finished product decided. Seed merchants can convert this to seed weights based on their experience of germination rates, and on the size of seed – both very variable parameters.

But how much seed should be sown or how dense should the planting be established? Views vary – not just based on science either. Some research has suggested that grassland seed mixes could be sown at rates as low as 4 or 10kg/ha (Stevenson *et al.*, 1995) whereas most seed suppliers recommend 30kg/ha. Some tree planting is still established at 1m densities, whereas woodland creation would benefit from wider spacing, better mixtures, and more random patterns. Seed merchants sell meadow mixes with around 80% grasses and 20% wildflower, yet this does not reflect the composition of many grasslands. The common denominator influencing these

Figure 2. Dorset Heathland – part of a cultural landscape which would have been interrelated with pasture and woodland – can we re-create such a landscape on this scale?

decisions is economics. Practitioners are usually constrained by available budgets, wildflowers are costly, and grass seed cheap by comparison. Some flowers are much cheaper than others, so more of these – the inevitable ox-eye daisy and knapweed, end up in seed mixes than is sometimes appropriate.

Then, how much of the seed or stock obtained is locally native? Good practitioners have always advocated using locally native sources of plants, and certainly seed mixes have advanced greatly since the early days in the beginning of the 1980s. However, most grass seed is not native, let alone local to your area, and it is extremely expensive, and much planting stock still emanates from the Netherlands or elsewhere. You could also ask 'what is native?' Is seed collected from your area, but grown en masse in a better climate in other parts of the world native? Presumably, historians have a similar problem sourcing local stone slates or other materials, let alone re-creating eighteenth century textiles, paint etc. within the modern Health and Safety and Planning constraints. And I haven't noticed many historic sites without electric lights and modern toilets!

CONCLUSIONS

So where does this leave us? First, we should not delude ourselves that we can re-create in its entirety something that is long established and of historical interest. Even our repairs will be set in the modern environmental conditions and current constraints. Many are constrained by our scientific knowledge, and fashioned by the flavour or thinking of the day. That does not mean that restoration and re-creation should not be attempted. It should, but with the

Figure 3. An ox-eye daisy meadow, with yellow rattle – typical of the 'easy to create' grasslands.

limitations made clear both to ourselves and others. There are enormous benefits of good restoration and re-creation in terms of engaging the public, providing a more attractive backcloth to our everyday lives for us and plants and animals, and gaining general and political support for a better environment in town and country. So, is restoration an art or a science? Perhaps it's more realistically the art of applying the available science under particular financial and social constraints.

Long may all these restoration and re-creation efforts continue.

REFERENCES

Anderson, P., Tallis, J.H. and Yalden, D.W. (1997) *Restoring Moorland: Peak District Moorland Management Phase III Report*. Peak Park Joint Planning Board, Bakewell.

Gilbert, O. and Anderson, P. (1998) *Habitat Creation and Repair*. OUP, Oxford.

Grime, J.P., Hodgson, J.G. and Hunt, R. (1998) *Comparative Plant Ecology: a functional approach to common British species*. Unwin Hyman, London.

Jordan, W.R. III and Packard, S. (1989) *Just a few oddball species: restoration practice and ecological theory*. In: *Biological Habitat Reconstruction* (Ed. Buckley, G.P.), pp.18-26, Belhaven Press, London.

Stevenson, M.J., Bullock, J.M. and Ward, L.K. (1995) Recreating semi-natural communities: Effect of sowing rate on establishment of calcareous grassland. *Restoration Ecology*, **3**, 279-289.

SUSTAINABLE DEVELOPMENT AND GREEN NETWORKS IN URBAN AND POST-INDUSTRIAL LANDSCAPES

John Box
Consultant and Principal Environmental Scientist

INTRODUCTION

Like air and water, biodiversity and natural landscapes are assumed to be a free resource that we take for granted and which can be adversely affected without direct economic payment. However, the protection and continued enjoyment of natural resources does entail costs to individuals and to society. Legislation, planning guidance and public attitudes are continually driving the burden of these costs away from the victim and the taxpayer and onto the consumer and the shareholder where they rightfully belong.

However, over the past forty years the conservation of nature in Europe has focussed on sites and the protection of rare habitats and species, rather than on the overall losses of biodiversity due to development pressures (whether from agriculture, forestry or built development). Wildlife legislation has not yet set limits for changes in species or populations in relation to the development of individual sites – either due to a change in the land-use of a site or to subsequent adverse impacts on wildlife in the vicinity of the site (such as noise, increased access, agricultural run-off, changes in local hydrology and water-flows). Sustainability may offer a more appropriate mechanism to achieve net gains in biodiversity for individual projects. Any project – industrial, residential, commercial, agricultural, mineral extraction, fisheries – can be assessed for biodiversity and sustainability.

TELFORD AND ITS GREEN NETWORK

The case study is the Green Network in Telford (Annex 1) which is of significance in a national context because all the green spaces in the town are included in the Green Network which is accorded formal recognition and protection in a Local Plan. The strength of the network is the multiple, overlapping purposes which include nature conservation, formal and informal recreation, an aesthetic and landscape context, and public access.

Telford is some 50 km to the west of Birmingham and was planned to create a new environment away from the West Midlands conurbation. It is a new town based on a number of existing settlements which from the early 1960s onwards have been extended and linked by major new housing, industrial and commercial areas.

The characteristic landscape of Telford has been formed by a unique integration of naturally regenerated former industrial areas with high-quality mass planting involving around 6 million trees and 10 million shrubs. This unusual combination of natural regeneration and landscape planting has resulted in a rich and complex post-industrial landscape where nature conservation is a significant land-use (Telford Development Corporation 1986). The dominant place of landscaping has given Telford a particularly green appearance and firmly established the original design concept of "The Forest City" which was originally articulated in the landscape structure plans produced by Telford Development Corporation in the 1970s.

The diversity of wildlife habitats is a direct result of the industrial history of Telford which has been subject to mining for coal, ironstone, clay and limestone over hundreds of years (Sinker et al., 1985; Box 1999). The last two centuries have seen these operations carried out on a scale sufficient to leave permanent reminders on the landscape. The pit mounds and spoil heaps which have re-vegetated with heather and woodland are well-loved and characteristic landscape features. They support a complex series of habitats which are the result of interactions between the chemistry of the various spoil materials and the age of the pit-mounds.

There is a hierarchy of nature conservation designations within and adjacent to Telford. Benthall Edge Wood (to the south), Lincoln Hill, Lydebrook Dingle (to the west), Muxton Marsh and New Hadley Brickpit are nationally important as Sites of Special Scientific Interest. There are three statutory Local Nature Reserves designated by Telford and Wrekin Council: the Town Park and associated wildlife areas, Granville which is also a nature reserve managed by the Shropshire Wildlife Trust and lies within a larger Country Park, and Limekiln Wood. The Shropshire Hills AONB starts in Telford and extends southwest from the town forming the link between the Green Network and the hills of the Wrekin and the Ercall and the wooded limestone escarpment of Wenlock Edge.

There are twenty-two *Wildlife Sites* identified by the Shopshire Wildlife Trust as being of county importance and recorded in the Environmental Record produced by the County Council. Additionally, there are thirty-six *Sites of Ecological Value*, a third-tier designation, which are recognised by Telford and Wrekin Council. The *Wildlife Sites* and the *SOEVs* are in a mixture of private and public ownership.

The Ironbridge Gorge forms the southern end of Telford with settlements on both banks of the River Severn which is spanned by the first iron bridge in the world (erected in 1779). Much of this area has been designated as a *World Heritage Site* by UNESCO because of the significance of the matrix of buildings, ancient monuments, open spaces and woodlands and associated with the start of the Industrial Revolution. The area is a major tourist attraction with a range of industrial monuments, including the extensive Blists Hill open-air museum with its Victorian shops and industrial buildings. The steep wooded slopes on both sides of the River Severn form a dramatic landscape and a rich wildlife corridor.

Much of the open space of Telford has been incorporated into its *Green Network* which provides a landscape framework with recreational, aesthetic and nature conservation functions (Rohde & Kendle 1997; Barker 1997). These multiple, often overlapping, functions are a fundamental part of its character and undoubtedly give it strength. Sites with particular nature conservation value (SSSIs, LNRs, and Wildlife Sites) lie within this network rather like plums in a pudding. The *Green Network* links with the surrounding countryside westwards to the distinctive hills of the Wrekin and the Ercall, southwest to Wenlock Edge, south to the River Severn, and north to the Weald Moors.

The *Green Network* covers some 2,300 ha and includes all the open areas of Telford which are of ecological, aesthetic and recreational value. Some 2,000 ha is in public ownership and there are open spaces in private ownership which make a valuable contribution to the network, for example golf courses, paddocks and fields. More than 45 miles of strategic and local footpaths make these areas accessible to local residents. Each individual piece of land in the *Green Network* is important in the contribution it makes to the overall functions of the whole network. Significantly, the *Green Network* holds the key to sustaining the attractiveness of Telford for residents, visitors and inward investors.

GREEN NETWORKS AND ENVIRONMENTAL FUNCTIONS

Green spaces, parks, wildspaces in urban areas are the places where the majority the population have their day-to-day contacts with wildlife. Research suggests that people derive considerable benefits from contact with nature (Rohde & Kendle, 1994). Therefore, ensuring adequate opportunities for people to come into contact with nature in their everyday lives should result in direct benefits to their health and happiness. By extension, the provision of accessible greenspace in urban areas should make these areas more acceptable to live in and help decrease the desire to move to "greener" surroundings elsewhere.

Fragmentation and isolation of wildlife habitats and greenspaces by the intensification of land-use (whether urban impacts, forestry, or agriculture), make nature vulnerable. A countervailing pressure against urban intensification can be supplied by linking individual sites with wildlife corridors or green corridors into a network of wildlife sites and open spaces which form the green framework of urban areas (Barker, 1997). Such a green network has the potential to contribute to minimum targets for the provision of urban greenspaces (Box & Harrison, 1993; Harrison et al., 1995). Planning within a framework of a green network allows both people and wildlife to benefit from connectivity in terms of both the overall landscape as well as the natural features. Green networks can function over a wide range of scales from a strategic integration of urban areas into the surrounding countryside through the local dimension right down to individual gardens.

Open sites in urban areas, particularly large ones, can have substantial environmental roles in absorbing rainfall and flood prevention, improving water quality and surface water discharges, ameliorating urban heat-island effects, and promoting airflows which can flush out atmospheric pollutants. These benefits tend to increase with the extent and structure of plant cover. Indeed, urban woodlands and wooded landscape features can reduce air pollution and noise. The retention of these important environmental functions needs to be considered during the urban development and redevelopment process particularly given the current focus on new housing on brown-field sites (Box & Shirley, 1999).

TELFORD LOCAL PLAN

The *Green Network* was first formally included in the *Telford Local Plan* covering the period 1991-2001 (adopted in 1993). The report of the Inspector from the Public Local Inquiry into objections to this plan (Planning Inspectorate, 1992) supported the general concept of the *Green Network* and stated:

"The importance of the concept's environmental thread cannot be over emphasized: part of it comprises not just the retention of ecological and wildlife interest with its links via corridors, woods and open space to other areas, important as that it is; but it also includes, significantly, the key to sustain the attractiveness of Telford itself, for residents, visitors and investors, as part of Telford's own investment in its future." (para. 10.31).

"Within that thread lies the potential provision of one of the largest scale, visually beneficial and informal recreation assets of any town in the country." (para. 10.32).

The key issues for the *Green Network* are the maintenance and enhancement of its recreational, aesthetic and nature conservation functions. The interweaving of open space and natural features with a developing urban fabric requires the resolution and management of new issues. There are pressures on the natural resources of the *Green Network* from pollution and eutrophication, public access, and even natural succession (open water, grasslands and heathlands will turn into scrub and woodland without intervention). Finally, there is only a finite amount of land within Telford. Telford is recognised as a regional growth point and competing land-uses will become greater in the next Plan period up to 2016.

The concept of the *Green Network*, and the aims and policies, were '*saved*' into the district-wide *Wrekin Local Plan 1995-2006* (adopted February 2000). The *Wrekin Local Plan* gives pride of place at the start to a chapter on environment which includes an excellent section on sustainable development. This deals with a number of key concepts such as stewardship & equity, carrying capacity, and replacement cost.

Protection of the *Green Network* is offered through policies which do not normally allow built development within the network. However, the *Local Plan* recognises the need for flexibility in a new town and there is a framework of sustainable development incorporating the *Green Network*. In exceptional circumstances, development may be permitted but only where this would contribute to the overall aims of the *Green Network* and be offset by

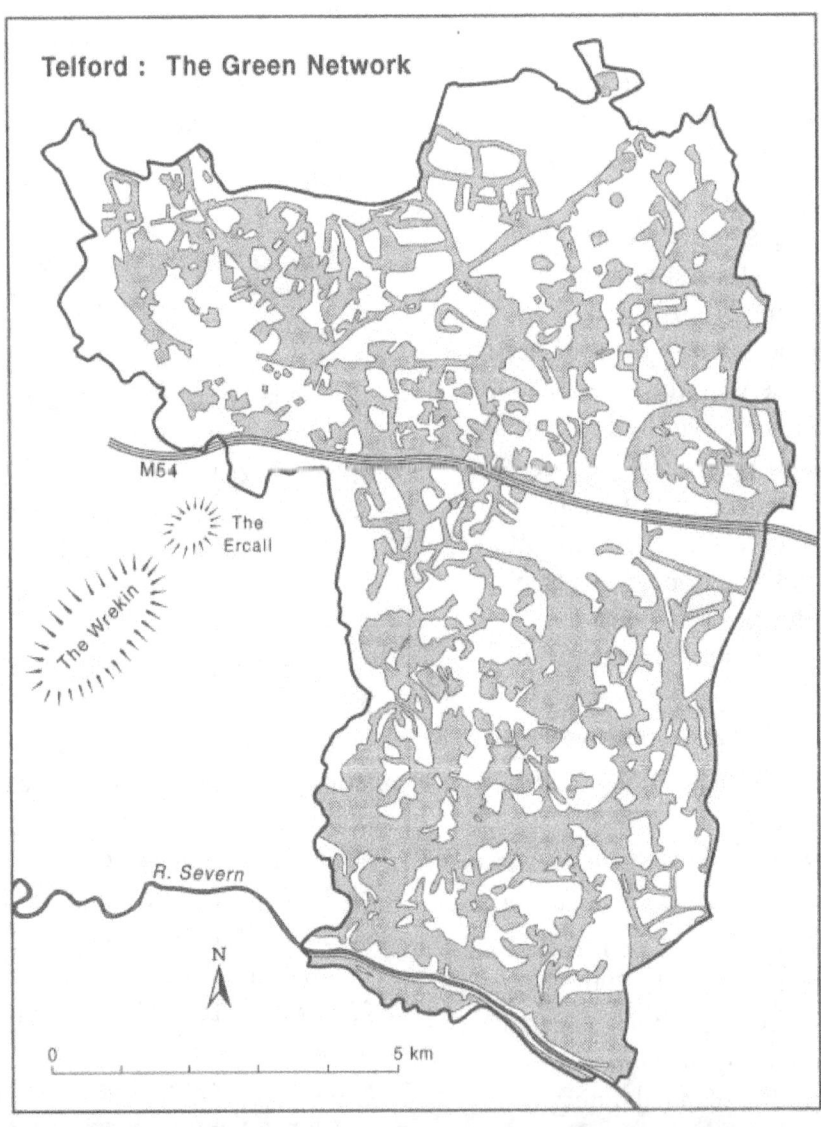

Figure 1. The Local Authority district of Telford showing its green network.

environmental and community benefits. Specific policies are included for the protection of the key sites of importance for nature conservation and the corridors and links between them.

Development in the *Green Network* may be permitted (*Policy OL4*) provided that:

- There are exceptional circumstances;
- It contributes or is complementary to the aims of the Green Network;
- Environmental and community benefits are an integral part of the proposal.

The supporting text to the policy gives examples of potential developments within the *Green Network* as well as examples of environmental and community benefits. Such treatment of sustainable development accords with the view of the *UK Round Table on Sustainable Development* that the planning system has the potential to be a fundamental instrument in the achievement of sustainable development and that sustainable development should be made a principal purpose of local authorities (*UK Round Table on Sustainable Development*, 2000).

SUSTAINABILITY MATRIX

Sustainable development – or sustainability – sounds good in theory but is very hard to get to grips with in practice. Defined as development which meets the needs of the present without compromising the ability of future generations to meet their own needs, sustainability has been likened to a *'three-legged stool'* whose legs comprise economic, social and environmental issues - with one leg missing, the stool will fall over and the project is not sustainable.

The effective planning and management of urban land is fundamental to any development strategy based on sustainability (Shirley & Box, 1999). *Policy OL4* and its supporting text in the *Wrekin Local Plan* may provide a planning framework but do not provide developers or planners with the tools to decide if projects are really sustainable in a way which is objective and transparent. The use of a *'Sustainability Matrix'* (Annex 2) could be of particular relevance in situations where development, redevelopment, or extensions to existing developments are proposed within the Green Network. The matrix makes use of the Government's *'Headline Indicators'* of sustainable development as set out in the White Paper on sustainable development *'A Better Quality of Life'* (DETR, 1999a) and developed in the subsequent baseline assessment which looked in more detail at the indicators (DETR,1999b).

The *Sustainability Matrix* allows the sustainability of a project – or projects - to be assessed against the '*Headline Indicators*' and put into three categories: Red, Amber, Green (Box, Brownjohn & Bason, 2000). Red issues are those which have a significant adverse effect on sustainability – these issues need to

Figure 2. The Sustainability Matrix

Headline Indicators		Effects of Development		
		Red	Amber	Green
Economic	Economic growth			
	Investment			
	Employment			
Social	Poverty & social exclusion			
	Educational qualifications			
	Life expectancy			
	Housing quality			
	Crime			
Environmental	Climate change			
	Air pollution			
	Road traffic			
	Water quality			
	Wild birds			
	Reusing previously developed land			
	Waste			

be addressed urgently. Amber ones give a warning – in other words, you must try harder. Green is for issues which contribute significantly to sustainability.

Given the function of the *Green Network* in Telford in terms of nature conservation, public amenity, and recreation, the assessment of the sustainability of a project and its contribution to environmental and community benefits, as required by the *Local Plan*, could make use of a wider set of relevant indicators, such as:

- The official headline indicators of biodiversity (wild bird populations) and water quality (rivers of good and fair quality) (DETR, 1999a) in conjunction with some of the supporting indicators which include access to open space (DETR, 1999b);

- Wider biodiversity indicators based on the national *Biodiversity Action Plan* and the *Shropshire Biodiversity Action Plan*;

- Measures of environmental services such as the variety and sizes of natural greenspace accessible to local communities (Box & Harrison, 1993; Harrison *et al.*, 1995; English Nature, 1996);

- Measures of environmental quality involving both people and wildlife such as the provision of Local Nature Reserves per thousand people in the population (Box & Harrison, 1993; English Nature, 1996).

CONCLUSIONS

The protection of the environmental assets within the *Telford Green Network* through the planning system has similarities with the use of the planning system by the authorities in the National Parks to protect their environmental assets. In both situations, there is a vision which recognises that the environment is an economic asset. The *Telford Green Network* demands the highest standards in relation to its management, enhancement and, in exceptional circumstances, development or redevelopment.

The *Green Network* offers a framework for conserving and enhancing all the green spaces in Telford, but only in the context of environmentally sustainable development. Sustainability is a cross-cutting issue which, for example, links control of surface water runoff with groundwater recharge and with wetland creation and biodiversity. The Sustainability Matrix is a tool that can identify and "quantify" the essential ingredients and critical factors of development proposals and can be used:

a) To compare different end-uses for a given site in terms of their contribution to sustainability; or

b) To audit a particular design for a proposed end-use to improve the overall sustainability of the project.

REFERENCES

Barker, G. (1997) A Framework for the Future: green networks with multiple uses in and around towns and cities. *English Nature Research Report*, **No. 256**, English Nature, Peterborough.

Box, J. (1999) Nature conservation and post-industrial landscapes. *Industrial Archaeology Review*, **XXI**, 137-146.

Box, J, Brownjohn, D and Bason, T. (2000) A gauge of success. Hednesford Brickworks reclamation: the sustainability matrix in action. *Sustain*, **1(2)**, 22-23.

Box, J. D. and Harrison, C. (1993) Natural spaces in urban places. *Town & County Planning*, **62**, 231-235.

DETR (1999a) *A Better Quality of Life: a strategy for sustainable development for the United Kingdom*. Cm 4345. The Stationery Office Ltd, London.

DETR (1999b) *Quality of Life Counts: indicators for a strategy for sustainable development for the United Kingdom: a baseline assessment*. Department of the Environment, Transport & the Regions, London.

English Nature (1996) *Nature is Good for You*. English Nature, Peterborough.

Harrison, C., Burgess, J., Millward, A. and Dawe, G. (1995) Accessible natural greenspace in towns and cities: a review of appropriate size and distance criteria. *English Nature Research Report*, **No.153**, English Nature, Peterborough.

Planning Inspectorate (1992) *Telford Local Plan: Report on Objections to the Plan. PINS/P3230/429/2*. The Planning Inspectorate, Bristol.

Rohde, C. L. E. and Kendle, A. D. (1997) Human well-being, natural landscapes and wildlife in urban areas: a review. *English Nature Science*, **No. 22**, English Nature, Peterborough.

Shirley, P. and Box, J. (1999) *Biodiversity, brownfield sites and housing: quality of life issues for people and wildlife*. Urban Wildlife Partnership, Newark.

Sinker, C. A., Packham, J. R., Trueman, I. C., Oswald, P. H., Perring, F. H. and Prestwood, W. V. (1985) *Ecological Flora of the Shropshire Region*. Shropshire Trust for Nature Conservation, Shrewsbury, pp.135-152.

Telford Development Corporation (1986) *Landscape Structure Plan and Nature Conservation Strategy*. Telford Development Corporation, Telford.

UK Round Table on Sustainable Development (2000) *Planning for Sustainable Development in the 21st Century*. UK Round Table on Sustainable Development, London.

LANDSCAPE LANDFORM SIMULATION: PEAK DISTRICT TRIALS

John Gunn
The Limestone Research Group, University of Huddersfield.

ABSTRACT PAPER

Prior to the middle of the twentieth Century most Peak District limestone quarries were relatively small and following the cessation of stone extraction the disused quarries generally merged into the landscape relatively quickly under the influence of natural processes of weathering and erosion and plant colonisation. However, the trend since the 1950's has been for working to be concentrated in increasingly large quarries with high rock faces and a multi-bench structure. The scale and extent of these modern quarries is much greater and current methods of stone excavation produce relatively straight faces which, if untreated, are likely to remain as conspicuous engineered features in the landscape for many decades or even hundreds of years. As the quarries are often in, or adjacent to, areas of high scenic value there is a conflict between demand for the mineral resource and the use of the surrounding area as a recreational / touristic resource.

During the late 1970's and early 1980's it became increasingly apparent that there was a need for techniques to reclaim the more visually obtrusive faces but few such techniques were available. The Limestone Research Group, using funding from the Department of the Environment and with the co-operation of quarry companies and explosives engineers, pioneered an innovative approach to quarry face restoration termed Landform Replication. This involves the use of novel methods of explosives engineering termed "Restoration Blasting" to construct new landforms that are subsequently selectively vegetated using Habitat Reconstruction techniques. Between 1988 and 1992, large-scale trials were carried out at two Derbyshire quarries, Tunstead and Hope. New landform assemblages comprising screes, buttresses and headwalls were constructed and the screes were then vegetated with a view to producing two habitat types, limestone grassland and broad leafed woodland.

Unfortunately, a short recession and re-organisation in the quarrying industry during the early 1990's meant that there was no aftercare of the establishing vegetation which suffered badly from a rabbit infestation. Nevertheless, following an independent technical audit of the work in 1993/4, it was concluded that restoration blasting and habitat reconstruction can be practical and visually acceptable techniques, if used in the right circumstances. The experimental sites were located within operational quarries and the project yielded practical lessons and theoretical insights of wider relevance to land reclamation practice. A further independent audit, designed to measure the long-term success of the work, was commissioned in October 1997.

It is important to recognise that the trials to date were designed to simulate the landform-vegetation assemblages developed over many thousand years in a specific part of the Peak District. As such they are not directly transferable to other areas. However, the landform application approach has been used successfully by other workers in Canada and it is suggested that the principles have wider applicability. Application to all faces in a large quarry would be prohibitively expensive but selective application to the more visually obvious faces should have positive environmental benefits.

STOWE: THE CONSERVATION OF A DESIGNED LANDSCAPE

Richard Wheeler
National Trust

INTRODUCTION

The gardens at Stowe have been described as the largest work of art in the UK; whether or not this is correct, they are certainly the most documented. Besides records in numerous county record offices, there are at least 300,000 documents in the Huntington Library in Pasadena. (The exact number is not known, a seemingly common fault for election year in the USA).

The full time involvement of the National Trust began in 1990 with a continuing programme of research and planning, running alongside initial clearance and site assessment. This research began with a report from Dominic Cole and Camilla Beresford of Land Use Consultants. The survey brought together all the then available information about Stowe, and sought to interpret this against a topographical survey of the whole site.

Following on from this plan, the Trust's Head of Gardens, Mike Calnan, was able to bring together the work of the Project Team into a 100-year Restoration and Management plan. These two documents together have informed the first stage restoration of the place.

However, the continuing research programme at the Huntington Library, and the evidence discovered by the National Trust's archaeologist working with the gardeners in this initial restoration, has refined our knowledge of the gardens. This has unlocked a large corpus of new information.

THE FRAMEWORK CONSERVATION PLAN

This information and its interpretation have been codified into a *Framework Conservation Plan* for the whole site: house, gardens and park. This plan does not seek to make decisions over restoration or management, but to provide all the information necessary to understand all aspects of the development of Stowe and their cultural significance. Following on from this master plan, a series of *Conservation Plans* for each character area is being prepared, and from these detailed restoration proposals are formulated.

In parallel with this plan the Property Manager has produced a five-year *National Trust Management Plan*. This details the day-to-day working of the property, and informs the annual *Implementation Plan*. The latter draws together all the work done by the staff on the property for the current year.

Lastly, the issue of new buildings in the landscape, for Stowe School, has been addressed by means of a *Development Plan*. This takes the form of Impact Assessment of these new buildings upon the imperatives that were forthcoming from the *Conservation Plan* work. For the future, we are now working on a planning framework that will meet the requirements of *World Heritage Site* status. This will have to include policies for staffing, access, interpretation, planning protection, and the treatment of areas within the *World Heritage Site*, but not in the ownership of the National Trust.

This paper deals with the conservation planning that is going into the work at Stowe, just one aspect of the significance of Stowe that fed into the planning work. This included research in the Stowe archive in Los Angeles, and in various British Record offices. Work involved:

- Transcription of gardening fortnightly accounts, clerk of works accounts, legal documents – conveyances, agreements, wills, tenancies, enclosure acts, letters, maps and plans, architects' documents, (very little direct bills etc., but written works on Vanbrugh, Kent, Gibbs, Borra and Valdre);

- Extractions from eighteenth century literature, - the writings of Addison, Lord Shaftesbury, Fielding and Congreve, classical allusions – Horace, Virgil, Catullus Urbaricus, etc.,

- Eighteenth century poetry – the works of Thompson, Glover, Pope, Hammond, Lyttelton and West,

- Extractions from eighteenth century politics – William Pitt the elder, Earl Temple, George Grenville, John Wilkes, William Pitt the younger, Wyndham Grenville, the first Duke of Buckingham, the second Duke as Marquess of Chandos;

- Extractions from writings on eighteenth century warfare - Lord Cobham and the wars in the Low Countries, Thomas Grenville and 1747 engagement off Cape Finisterre, the Seven Years War in Canada, the West Indies, West Africa, India and Europe.

All this leads to an understanding of Stowe that goes way beyond the relative positions of plants, trees paths and buildings.

THE WHIGS AND THEIR IDEALS

Stowe had always been intensely serious, and the moral ideas of vice and virtue were inextricably entwined with the political ideals of the time. In terms of restoration these themes need to be unravelled and understood. This paper follows just the political and virtuous themes today. In 1713, when Richard Temple, Lord Cobham one of Marlborough's generals, returned flush with success from the French wars, the only political ideal was *Grand Whiggery*. The Tories had had their final apotheosis under Queen Anne and had been reduced to a Jacobite rump, destined to be out of office for half a century. So until 1760 and the accession of George III, the country was ruled by the great Whig families, and Lord Cobham and his extended family of Temples and Grenvilles considered themselves to be the guardians of the Whig morality, with Stowe as its shrine.

So what were these great ideals? Central was *liberty*. The Whigs considered themselves the successors in title to the libertarian thinkers and soldiers of the previous century, who had struggled against the Stuarts, Raleigh, Hampden and of course William of Orange. The Glorious Revolution in 1688 had laid down the ground rules for a constitutional monarchy, and this was further codified by the Hanoverian succession with its first incumbent rather conveniently speaking no English. And this *succession* can be put down as the second of the Whig ideals.

Thirdly, there was the *constitution*. In the eyes of the Whigs, only a small amount of rationalisation was needed to trace our constitution back to our Saxon or Gothic ancestors, with their supposed love of Liberty, their parliament, the Witan, and their system of electing the King. This last the most important.

The fourth ideal concerned *religion*. This was not so much in the question of belief or liturgy, but far more in keeping the protestant succession of these supposedly malleable Hanoverians, rather than the turbulent Stuarts, with their unhelpful ideas of the Divine Right of Kings.

Lastly I am going to include the prosecution of the wars against the French. For the second time there was an informal Hundred Years War with the Old Enemy. During the eighteenth century the years of peace with France could be counted on the fingers of one hand.

So where does all this leave Stowe? The story actually begins with the second of these Whig ideals, the Hanoverian Succession. Cobham's title came from a grateful King, the first of these Hanoverians, George I. So his equestrian statue took pride of place on the North Front of the house. And since he had no Queen; she had been divorced and left locked up in Hanover, his familial example had to be expressed by son George Augustus, and daughter in law Caroline. These two took the gardens to the south of the house while the King had the Park. All this is quite simple. But in the 1730s, the iconography became more subtle and forward looking. Gilbert West, one of Lord Cobham's nephews, and one of the minor poets of the eighteenth century wrote a topographical poem on Stowe which gives us a taste of the intention. The 'Good Old King' in his original position at Stowe is in the guise of Marcus Aurelius, that most worthy of Roman Emperors, and is leading his files of soldiers, represented by the two great avenues of trees on either side:

> *Far o'er the level green in just array*
> *long rows of trees their adverse*
> *fronts display*
> *high on a mount amid a verdant field*
> *behold the good old king in armour*
> *clad*

But the plot becomes more subtle. Control of a constitutional monarch by the great Whig families was central to the scheme of government envisaged by the Glorious Revolution, and the inscription on King George's plinth reflected this: '*In medio mili Caesar erit / In viridi campo de marmore ponam/ propter aquam.......*' '*In the middle (of my garden) I will have the imperial Caesar.....*'.

The point was made by the omission of the second half of the first line: '*... templumque tenebit*'. Thus: '*In the middle of my garden I will have Caesar ...**and he will have Temple**'.* In other words Richard Temple, Viscount Cobham, behind the throne, in the position of power. The ambitions of the Whig oligarchy for this constitutional monarch were set out in Nelson's Seat (1719, but also named in the 1730s, The Roman Temple) situated at the eastern end of Nelson's Walk, on its apex with Roger's Walk and with its inscriptions from the Constantine Arch: (in translation): '*Having extended his power beyond the Euphrates and the Tigris, as far as the ocean, this most potent Prince, assigns the Empire of the World to Rome.*' and from the Capitol: '*after the death of Lucius Verus, partner in the Empire with Marcus, Rome conferred upon him, the Empire of the World.*'

Nelson's Walk was extended in 1724 beyond Lees' Bastion, its original terminus, to James Gibbs' Roman Pavilion, or Boycott Pavilion, built as one of a pair flanking Kent's original entrance gates to the park. One was an open belvedere in the gardens, and the other a house for Cobham's comrade in arms, Colonel Sam Speed, in the park. This Roman Pavilion again strengthened the Roman iconography with statues of Cicero, **the** great Republican, and Marcus Aurelius again. With these two, but presumably of less iconographic significance were Livia and Faustina. These statues were described as being of lead, painted to look like bronze. These three together then, Roman Pavilion, Nelson's Seat, and the statue of George I, delineated the ambition of Lord Cobham and others of the Whig oligarchy to develop an empire to rival that of Ancient Rome, an ambition achieved fifteen years later by his nephew (-in-law), William Pitt.

NEXT LIBERTY

Poets were regular visitors to Stowe, and their work intermingled with that of the politicians. James Thompson, of 'Rule Britannia' fame was one such, and had written an epic poem on the progress of Liberty from her beginnings in the Ancient World to her final and true home, in the Britain of the eighteenth century. Whether his poem was influenced by the iconographic programme at Stowe, or *vice versa* can never be known, but the similarity between the themes is quite apparent.

Thompson tells us that Liberty had her first awakenings in Egypt and the Middle East, so this was represented at Stowe by that icon of Egypt, the Obelisk. Situated in the Fallow Deer Park, it formed the apex of a great triangle with its base upon the gardens earlier boundary, shown on Sarah Bridgeman's 1739 plan of Stowe. Egypt, however, was not somewhere for Liberty to linger. Thompson tells us: '*For Greece my sons of Egypt I forsook*', and so the next station on the progress was a Grecian Valley and Temple: '*The promised land of arts… Unrival'd Greece*'. The Grecian Temple, later rededicated by Earl Temple to Concord and Victory, was an attempt by Lord Cobham to recreate a temple of the Ancient World, set in its Attic landscape: '*In Attic bounds hence heroes, sages, wits, Shone thick as stars, the Milky Way of Greece*'. From this Grecian Valley, though, Liberty fled, after the final defeat of the Greeks by Philip of Macedon at the Battle of Cheronaea: '*Thus tame submitted to the victor's yoke. Greece, once the gay, the turbulent, the bold…*'

Thompson's synopsis (or 'argument') for the next chapter describes how the 'spirit of Liberty' finds its place in Rome via the Grecian colonies of southern Italy, the consequent petty republics, and finally the great Roman Republic. At Stowe, we are told by Lady Newdigate, visiting in 1748, that Rome was to be represented by an amphitheatre replicating that at Verona, a triumphal arch, and a column in imitation of that of the Emperor Trajan. Sadly the proposed amphitheatre was never to be, although its site was probably to have been at the end of the Grecian valley, and the idea of the Triumphal Arch was taken by Cobham's nephew and heir, Earl Temple, to the South Vista as the Corinthian Arch. However, the imitation of Trajan's Column was erected, on the Grecian Diagonal, designed by James Gibbs, and built with modifications by the Head Gardener and Clerk of Works, Lancelot Brown. Looking very little like its supposed model, it was commissioned by Lady Cobham in honour of her husband.

So Lord Cobham's place at the head of this libertarian crusade was secured by the erection of his statue, in the guise of a Roman Imperator, at the top of this column. The inscription, now superseded, was the (misquoted) line from that greatest of Roman republicans, Cicero:

> '*Quatenus nobis denegatur diu ivere,*
> *Relinquamus aliquid,*
> *Quo nos vixisse testemur.*'

('As we cannot live long /Let us leave something behind us/ To shew that we have lived.')

And from his lofty vantage point, Cobham was able to look down the Grecian diagonal to the Grecian Temple, and down the Gothic Walk to Gibbs' Gothic Temple.

If we return though, to Thompson's poem, of course Liberty in Rome was doomed by the death of Brutus, and rule by a series of despotic emperor. Thompson tells us that:

> '*From Rome the Goddess of Liberty goes among the northern nations; where, by infusing into them her spirit and general principles, she lays the groundwork of her future establishments; sends them in vengeance on the Roman Empire, now*

totally enslaved; and then, with the arts and the sciences in her train, quits earth during the dark ages.'

The fourth part of Thompson's poem then rehearses the progress of Liberty through British history, from the defeat of Caractacus and Boadicea by the Romans, the departure of the legions in AD 426, and through successive invasions by Saxons, Danes and finally the tyrannical rule of the Normans:

*'The haughty Norman seized at once an isle,
For which, through many a century, in vain,
The Roman, Saxon, Dane, had toiled and bled.
Of Gothic nations this the final burst.'*

Two buildings at Stowe commemorate those Gothic nations, with their love of Liberty. The first, the Gothic Temple, an ironstone building set on the edge of the Hawkwell Field, and surrounded by wild, uncultivated (and therefore libertarian landscape) is described in the early guidebooks as dedicated to *'The Liberty of our Ancestors'*. Approached by the Thanet Walk, it reminds us that our liberties stem from our Gothic ancestors, those freedom loving tribes of Northern Europe, who landed on the island of Thanet, bringing our *'Old Gothic Constitution'* to Britain. Lord Cobham himself traced his descent from the Saxon Earls of Mercia, hence the ceiling of the Gothic Temple is decorated with the armorial shields shewing this pedigree, and makes the point that the great Whig families were the rightful defenders of Liberty. The point is accentuated by the inscription from Corneille's *Horace* over the door (then):

'Je rends graces aux Dieux de nestre pas Romain.'

(I thank God for not being a Roman.)

And around the Temple were placed the seven deities of the Saxon world which gave their names to the days of the week; thus Sunna, Mona, Tiw, Woden, Thuna, Frigga and Seater.

The second was a circular building in the form of a medieval Tower house. Set outside the gardens as an eye-catcher, it did double duty as the lodge for the keeper of the deer in the Park. (It was rededicated in the nineteenth century as the Bourbon Tower). Thompson had no higher opinion of the Normans than he had of the Roman emperors, and compares them unfavourably with the last Saxon king before Harold's defeat at Hastings:

*Instead of Edward's equal gentle laws,
The furious victor's partial will prevailed.*

It was not until the time of King John that the Barons formed, the first confederacy...in defence of the nation's interest against the King:

*'The Barons next a nobler league began,
Both those of English and of Norman race,
In one fraternal nation blended now,
The nation of the free'.*

James Gibbs designed the third, then, of his buildings of Liberty, Stowe Castle. Built as a great curtain wall hiding a farmhouse, set on the horizon a mile from the gardens, it provides the most spectacular of the eye-catchers at Stowe. Meanwhile inside the gardens, looking up the Hawkwell Field, is Gibbs' Temple of Friendship; filled with the busts of those defenders of Liberty, the Prince of Wales, Lord Cobham and their political allies. Next Stowe gives us the exemplars of the Whig philosophy, in the *Ancient World*, and in Thompson's *'land of the free'*.

Whosoever the author of Stowe's Elysian Fields, the importance of the place was the decision not to try and formalise something intrinsically informal. The topography was accepted as it was and embellished it with an essay in morality taken straight from the pages of the Tatler. This was an allegory by Addison, published in January 1709 describing temples of Honour, Virtue, and Vanity in Elysium, the heaven of the ancients. To Cobham with his group of nephews to advise, this, together with an earlier Addison essay on the Choice of Hercules, fitted perfectly with the new iconography of the garden: the choice between Vice and Virtue.

Just as in the Addison essay therefore, the entrance to the garden lay along *'A great road ....terminated by the Temple of Virtue.'* At Stowe this was the Great Cross Walk, running from Lee's Bastion, and bounding the parterre, before terminating in the trees beside the old church, at Kent's Temple of Ancient Virtue, inhabited by the four moral exemplars of the ancient world, Homer, Socrates, Epaminondas and Lycurgus. In the essay this temple obscures the view to the Temple of Honour, so at Stowe the equivalent Temple of the British Worthies is set across the river and only comes into view as one passes Ancient Virtue, and looks down into the valley. Finally Addison describes his Temple of Vanity, *'filled with hypocrites, pedants, freethinkers, and prating politicians; with a rabble of those who have only titles to make them great men'*. The temptation at Stowe, with the intentionally ruined Temple of Modern Virtue, to take a swipe at Sir Robert Walpole, perceived by Cobham's faction of nephews as a traitor to Liberty and all the ideals of Grand Whiggery, was far too great, and the temple was adorned, at least until 1769 with a statue of a headless trunk. It may well be that Alexander Pope had a hand in the interpretation of Addison's essay, and his own poem entitled *Fame*, he distinguishes between those to whom fame comes naturally, and those who seek after it. So his eighteenth century iconography (Susan Gordon) would have seen this statue as a reference to the headless body of Priam in the Aeneid, and whilst the Roman reader of Virgil's time might have taken this as a reference to Pompey, the Stowe visitor may well have taken the view that it represented Sir Robert, who was quite definitely one of the seekers after fame.

Following the walk therefore, past Ancient and Modern Virtue, the path leads down the hill, and crosses the Worthies River by way of William

Kent's Shell Bridge, in fact just a dam and spillway with a parapet only on the downstream side. Beyond the bridge one then comes to the British Worthies themselves, eight men of letters, and seven men and one woman of action, led to the Elysian Fields, *campos ducit ad Elysios*, by Mercury, the messenger of the gods, whose bust was placed in the oval niche above them.

But the timing of the Elysian Fields coincided with Lord Cobham turning against his party leader (and first Prime minister) Sir Robert Walpole, over the excise bill, and he was stripped of his colonelcy and became Sir Robert's bitterest enemy. Whilst remaining a Whig he considered that it was his duty to uphold the principles of Grand Whiggery, and he formed his own opposition grouping within the party. Variously known as the Whig Patriots, the Grenville cousinhood or Cobham's cubs, they later became the Grenville faction which wielded immense power in the Commons for three quarters of a century. They mostly comprised Cobham's nephews and nephews in law and included the Grenville brothers, Gilbert West, and William Pitt, and their political and poetaster friends, Alexander Pope, James Thompson, James Hammond, and they grouped themselves around the alternative court of the Prince of Wales, poor Fred. And the temptation was too great not to make a quite subtle political statement. So most of the panegyrics inscribed above these great men, are ill-concealed attacks on Walpole's government. So the bust of Alfred the Great, the mildest, most just, most munificent of Kings, everything that king George II was not, and beside him Edward the Black Prince the terror of Europe the delight of England, everything to which Prince Frederick aspired. And then of course in the temple of vanity over the river was Sir Robert himself.

Above the Shell Bridge the River Styx, or Alder River, overhung with ivy-clad and dead trees forms a closed and gloomy canopy. Certainly forming the counterpoint to the Elysian Fields, a place of happiness like the Isles of the Blest, perhaps it was intended as a depiction of Tartarus, the place of punishment. Here was found, first, the Temple of Contemplation and at the head of the valley Kent's Grotto. This was a fantastic and ornate rococo building covered inside and out with shell work, flanked by two diminutive (shell and pebble) rotundas, and housing a copy of the Crouching Venus. To one side of this part of the gardens and standing out into the Hawkwell Field was a small pond upon which the Chinese House was placed on wooden stilts. Whether it was an exemplar of Confucian virtue, a newly popular theme in the 1730s, or an aesthetic fancy, this building was the first of its type in England. It was hugely influential.

CONCLUSION

Finally, running through the whole of the garden is the ideal of the prosecution of the war against the old enemy. The only family member to get a place in the Elysian Fields is Thomas Grenville, a naval captain killed in

Ansons action against the French fleet off Finisterre in 1747. His column is surmounted by one of the muses driven from the parterre - Heroic Poetry, and she is reading from her scroll, *'non nisi grandia canto, heroic deeds alone my theme'*.

But two years later in 1749 Cobham died, leaving his most ambitious project, the Grecian Temple incomplete. The baton was picked up by Earl Temple, who immediately altered the design of the building to make it more nearly Grecian, by forming a pronaos and blocking the windows. But his main and most important alteration was to come in 1763 when he rededicated the building to Concord and Victory to celebrate his brother-in-law, Pitt's, great triumphs in the Seven Years War. 1759 had been the *annus mirabilis*, with victories in Canada, India and the West Indies, and Pitt and Temple had been keen to continue with this winning streak. But the new King George III, with his mentor the Earl of Bute, was determined upon a peace. Following serious disagreement with Pitt over the reported entry of Spain into the war, Pitt resigned and Temple with him. A deeply dishonourable peace was then agreed by the Duke of Bedford in 1762, and this was ratified in 1763. Temple was furiously angry and set John Wilkes with his eighteenth century *Private Eye, the North Briton*, upon the government, with devastating results. At Stowe he sublimated his passion with the Temple of Concord and Victory.

The building of the Triumphal Arch had been abandoned soon after its commencement in 1752, and Temple took the idea to a new and much more imposing site on the main axis from the South Front, and this became the Corinthian Arch. The obelisk in the park was rededicated to General Wolfe the victor of Quebec, one of the victories in the *annus mirablis* of the war. The composition was thus complete when the visitor could stand on the steps of Concord and Victory, and look one way to one of the military architects of victory, and the other to the (late) political architect of that victory, Lord Cobham.

WILDLIFE AND COAL - THE NATURE CONSERVATION VALUE OF POST-MINING SITES IN YORKSHIRE

Ian D. Rotherham, Jeff Lunn*, and Frank Spode

Sheffield Hallam University and English Nature*

INTRODUCTION

Much of the historical wealth of the South Yorkshire region and indeed of the whole Yorkshire Coalfield was derived from its resources of coal, ironstone and water. The extraction of minerals, coupled with urbanisation, has led to the naturally rolling landscape now dominated by cities, towns and villages, but still set within large areas of open countryside.

The geology of the region includes one of Britain's most important coalfields (Edwards & Trotter, 1954), and this continues to support a range of mining activities. At various times, the land within the Coal Measures Series has been worked for fireclay, ganister, pottery clay, lead, ironstone, mudstones and shales for brick manufacture, and stone (building materials, flags, grindstones). On the Permian and Triassic strata (which overlie Coal Measures the 'concealed coalfield'), lime, building sand and gypsum have been mined, with small amounts of barytes and oil. Sand has been extracted to provide silica for glassmaking, and gravel has also been worked and peat has also been opencast (Mitchell & Bromehead, 1947). However, these mining activities have been relatively minor compared with coal mining and the massive impact that it has had on the area.

The wildlife of the South Yorkshire region reflects its landscape characteristics. This changes with decreasing altitude from west to east, from the blanket bogs and upland heaths of the Pennines, through the rolling landscape of the coalfields, (partly urban and suburban and partly agricultural with complex mosaics of woodland, grassland and wetland) to an increasingly arable landscape with major lowland raised mires out towards the upper reaches of the Humber Estuary. Within this environmental resource the impacts of industrial activity are very significant.

This paper examines the effects of the mining industry on wildlife in the region, based on a study of seventy sites (Lunn, 2000), and the on-going work of the *South Yorkshire Biodiversity Research Programme* (See Rotherham, 1999 for example). A preliminary account was published by Lunn and Wild in 1995, and more recently key issues have been highlighted by Middleton (2000). Is this interaction of industry and landscape a case of complete devastation, or has mining activity unexpectedly allowed some wildlife to flourish?

The surprisingly positive contribution to local biodiversity of an environmentally positive restoration scheme has recently been highlighted by Lunn & Rotherham (2000). This particular site at Tankersley in Barnsley, now monitored for ten years after restoration, is described with reference to key groups of fauna and flora. These are particularly higher plants of ancient woods and meadows, and aquatic fauna such as amphibians and Odonata. This is even more interesting in the light of recent observations by Middleton (2000), concerning the high nature conservation value of many post-coaling sites in the South Yorkshire region, and the fact that this interest is often unrecognised and ignored in restoration schemes.

Lunn & Rotherham (2000) address the often contentious issues of opencast coal mining in Green Belt countryside, with particular reference to the North Derbyshire and South Yorkshire Coalfields. These are matters of frequently heated public debate as highlighted recently by Beynon *et al.* (2000). They focus on a small opencast coal mining project on land to the south-west of Barnsley, and consider the role of local people and a sympathetic planning system, in achieving major benefits for conservation. The need to facilitate such environmental benefits, and the potential for site restoration projects, are critically examined.

The positive and pro-active role of the local community in identifying the opportunity, and in turning words into actions, is discussed. The need for more effective monitoring of projects of this sort is emphasised.

With particular reference to opencasting, Beynon *et al.* place the social and political aspects of this industry into a wider context of the issues raised by widespread opencast coal mining that was occurring during the 1980s. In Chapter 6: *'Democracy! What democracy?* (pp 143-166), they cover the ground in great detail. They note the decline of employment based on extraction and processing in the region (from 40,000 to 13,000 jobs between 1975 and 1988 in Sheffield's Lower Don Valley alone). This was along with a legacy of dereliction and despondency. In Sheffield, one response was to spark a new phase of 'greening' of the landscape combined with economic regeneration. From a nature conservation perspective, this could be a mixed bag (as discussed by Rotherham, Cartwright and Watts, 2000), with ecologically interesting sites swept away to be replaced by green grass and lollipop trees!

Tinsley Park for example was 'found' as an urban wildlife site of major proportions in the 1980s, and scheduled as a *'Local Nature Site'* in the *Sheffield Nature Conservation Strategy* (Bownes *et al.*, 1991); the site was immediately under threat of total destruction. (Even now as noted by Middleton (2000) many post-industrial sites such as former colliery areas are being 'tidied up' often with little awareness or regard for any acquired conservation interest). Linked to the proposals to clean up the contaminated Tinsley Park site was the idea of a Sheffield Airport, and that this could be a cornerstone of Sheffield's regeneration. This idea was actively promoted by British Coal Opencast. They saw the opportunity to extract coal before the reserves were sterilised by new development. However, the outcomes of ecological surveys, of links to environmentally aware individuals in the Tinsley Action Group, and the enlightened approach of City Council officers and some politicians, ensured a more positive approach to the environmental issues. This was further sharpened when Mel Jones and Ian Rotherham highlighted the links to the medieval deer park and coppice woods and the presence still of the park banks and ditch. Some of these issues were reported in the environmental statement by Shepheard, Epstein & Hunter (1990), by Rotherham (1988) and Rotherham & Boon (1988).

These issues of nature conservation, of historic landscapes and their associated wildlife and cultural values are factors that underpin the thrust of this present paper.

CONTEMPORARY MINING METHODS AND IMPACTS ON WILDLIFE

Opencasting and deep-mining are the two major methods of coal extraction.

OPENCASTING

Opencast mining operations involve the use of heavy, earthmoving equipment to remove the strata above the coal to gain direct access to the reserves (British Coal Opencast, 1991). Those seams relatively close to the surface and generally too shallow to be worked by deep-mine methods, are worked, and the precision of modern machinery allows most of the coal to be extracted, sometimes including the pillar and stall systems left behind by old deep mines. The method is relatively new, beginning in 1942 as a wartime expedient, but has rapidly grown with the advent of new technology, especially the introduction of powerful and efficient machinery.

New sites are subject to a process of detailed planning and planning consents before exploitation. Reserves are proved through the production of a geological profile based on core samples recovered by drilling and borehole logging devices. Computer models accurately assess the coal reserves as well as the amounts of other materials such as mudstones, seat-earths, peat and other surface deposits including sub- and top-soils which have to be used in the process. Permissions and authorisations have to be secured if mining is to proceed (Anon., 1994b), and this includes the preparation of an Environmental Assessment and detailed restoration plans.

Screening mounds are established as a first step in the operation that progresses in a series of steps removing and storing the overburden before extracting the minerals. Restoration is normally to original ground levels and may incorporate features not present in the original landscape. Once sites have been secured, stripping of topsoil and subsoil using motor scrapers and mechanical shovels begins and these are stored separately and carefully for later use. Typical sites cover an area of about 200 ha have an average depth of 82 metres and contain 2.2 million tonnes of coal in a dozen seams of coal (British Coal Opencast, 1991). Around 40 tonnes of overburden are produced for each tonne of coal extracted. On some sites, old spoil-heaps are also re-worked and material may be processed through a washery plant to yield clean coal.

Restoration proceeds by the replacement of the overburden which is compacted in layers to generate the agreed landform in the restoration plan. Subsoil placed on top of the overburden is ripped to aid drainage, and topsoil application is managed under MAFF supervision for a five year period to monitor restoration of fertility to agricultural end-uses. The majority of restorations have been agricultural, but increasingly other uses such as forestry, amenity and 'infrastructural' development have taken place. Whilst restoration to a nature conservation end-use is now legitimate (Anon., 1993a), no such restorations purely to this end use were encountered in the core study. This said, some schemes included the provision of lakes and ponds designed to incorporate wildlife requirements.

DEEP MINING

Deep mining methods are long established in the region and have developed as technology has advanced. Coal and iron has been mined from the early Middle Ages, with early references at Hipperholme (Halifax) in 1274 and numerous small concerns in the Wakefield-Pontefract-Barnsley areas (Hey, 1986). Until the late eighteenth century, extraction methods were relatively simple, the minerals being won from outcrops near to the surface and which could be accessed by shallow pits and adits. 'Bell-pits' where shafts were sunk to access the reserves and waste material raised to the surface and dumped provided a larger scale operation but still involved no machinery, though the spoil-heaps created by this method can still be dramatic, such as the Elmley and Tankersley ironstone mines (Jones, 1995).

The study area was at the forefront of new winding and haulage technology from the early 1800's, when increasingly large pits could access deeper seams of coal. The early mines tended to be to the west of the study area and relatively small, but dramatic changes occurred from 1850. Output was then about 8 million tons *per annum* rising to over 73 million tons by 1913 (Hey, 1986). New settlements were created, as well as rapid development of existing small villages, as 'pit-villages' to house the labour required to meet the rise in demand. Many of the larger pits in the 'concealed' coalfield to the east were established in the twentieth century, with the last major group of pits to be developed - at Selby - receiving planning permission in 1976.

Early methods produced relatively little waste material, as the coal was immediately separated by hand on site, literally at the coal-face to avoid the need to handle waste material. However, modern and more efficient mechanised methods raised both coal and seat-earths along with parts of the seam roof. They are separated at the surface, with the waste material dumped on site. These spoil-heaps can be extensive, accumulating from years of tipping and can be dramatic in terms of visual and environmental impact. Spontaneous combustion can also be a problem in some older tips, but since the 1930's the separation techniques have improved greatly with the introduction of large-scale washing and settlement of tailings and slurry in lagoons (Richards, Moorhead & Laing Ltd., 1996).

Early spoil tips were not subject to any special treatment, and many have established a full vegetation cover through natural colonisation. However, many others, particularly those in active operation over the last 30-40 years, are huge and present large areas of land with little or no vegetation cover at all.

In recent years the deep mine coal industry has contracted substantially (the last active coal mine in Barnsley, once the centre of the coal industry, closed in 1993), and with this closure is associated a substantial legacy of redundant collieries, coal stocking ground and spoil heaps. Much effort, especially over the last decade, has been directed at 'restoring' this type of land (e.g. City of Wakefield, 1991), backed by a substantial regulatory framework and financial incentives, including the establishment of a specific agency, Regional Development Agency (subsuming English Partnerships), as facilitator. The reduction in the deep-mine industry has also been paralleled by an increase in opencasting (Hudson & Sadler, 1990).

It is obvious that mining, whether carried out by deep-mine or opencast methods, has a dramatic effect on existing landscapes, and that the large-scale development of collieries and spoil-heaps completely alters the existing landscape through the complete removal and replacement of surface ecosystems and subsurface strata.

Since much of the development of collieries in particular pre-dates any regulation requiring an assessment of the nature conservation interest of the land, few data are available to help quantify the loss of wildlife habitats or to help assess the value these may have had in a modern protected wildlife site system. However, examination of historical maps (such as the *First Edition Ordnance Survey c.1830-1840*) can provide evidence for the loss of some wildlife habitats presently considered of high value (such as ancient woodlands). In the study area, examples include New Park Spring, Grimethorpe, and Gawber Wood, Barnsley, both of which were known for the presence of rare species such as

Herb Paris *Paris quadrifolia*, and Nightingales *Luscinia megarhynchos* in the 1800s. Other marshland and wetland habitats have also been lost, such as along the River Aire wetlands (Brook, 1976), Ferrymoor at Grimethorpe and Killamarsh Meadows (just into Derbyshire) near Sheffield.

Two other major impacts of mining on local ecology and sites of nature conservation interest are the effects of mine-water discharges from old and abandoned collieries into watercourses, and the effects of subsidence. Mines also have an immediate impact on wetland areas through massive drainage and lowering of water-table due to pumping from deep-mines. On abandonment, this process may be reversed as pumps are switched off, and the now contaminated water rises once again. However, due to below ground disruption, and associated fracturing of rock strata, this rising water-table may behave differently from that which preceded it.

MINEWATERS

Water enters most mines in Britain and is normally actively removed through pumping. The chemical nature of these waters is variable but many, including those within the study area, contain reduced iron minerals which on contact with air, oxidise and precipitate out ferruginous deposits. Strata containing up to 10 % iron pyrites (ferrous sulphide), can dissolve on contact with air drawn down by the pumping, to produce sulphuric acid. This in turn leaches other metals such as cadmium, copper and zinc. Rates of oxidation can also be increased by the catalytic activity of bacteria such as *Thiobacillus*. Waters can also be saline due to the presence of dissolved chloride and sulphate salts leading to the establishment of brackish water habitats.

At working mines, waters such as these are treated by neutralisation, the settlement of solids and polishing through reed-beds before regulated discharge to watercourses, as water of good quality. However, long-abandoned mines can still produce polluting discharges and around such 100 discharges affecting 198 km of watercourses were estimated by the National Rivers Authority in 1994 (National Rivers Authority, 1994). These included some of the most damaging in the study area e.g. Sheephouse Wood and Bullhouse Colliery on the upper stretches of the Rivers Don and Little Don. Effluents here have levels of iron up to 75 mg/l, and in conjunction with the large volumes of discharge, produce a covering of ferric oxide deposits for around four km downstream of these rivers resulting in reductions of the macro-invertebrate populations and very low fish populations.

In general terms, the ecological effects of these waters (through both physical and chemical interaction) can include the depletion of numbers of pollution-sensitive organisms; reduction in biodiversity; depletion in numbers and biodiversity of the macro-invertebrate community; loss of spawning gravels for fish reproduction and nursery streams; and fish mortalities.

SUBSIDENCE

Subsidence of land surfaces occurs when and where deep-mines operate. Once the coal horizons are taken out, the worked areas left behind are allowed to collapse, causing a reduction in the surface of the land above. The amount of predicted subsidence can be calculated, and patterns are predictable with maximum levels immediately above the working seams, declining in a diminishing 'zone of influence' to zero.

Effects can be considerable, particularly on hydrology, including impact at local (site) and regional scales. One of the environmental features associated with large mines in the Yorkshire coalfield, is the creation of new wetlands caused by inundation of subsided areas. These are often in the floodplains of rivers, and some historical changes have been documented (Brook, 1976). Many of the natural floodplains along major rivers of the study area were regularly inundated. This flooding of largely 'grassland' areas was associated with the Norse term '*ings*'. Their agricultural management was characteristic, and often included the hay meadow systems, elements of which can still be found along other Yorkshire rivers e.g. the Derwent Ings. Areas would also have been managed as marsh and fen – providing hay, seasonal grazing, fuel, small wood, rushes, wildfowl, and fish, along with other products. The consequence of mining has been to create additional and often permanent (but sometimes temporary) flooding with consequential development of wetland ecosystems e.g. Fairburn Ings, Mickletown Ings, Broomhill Ings, Denaby Ings and Catcliffe Flash.

SMALLER WATER FEATURES

Also of value in the abandoned complexes of many mining sites, are the numerous small ponds and lagoons. Often these are excellent and locally important sites for amphibians, for grass snakes and for Odonata. Unfortunately, as 'derelict' sites, they often receive only scant recognition and little if any protection.

CHARACTERISTICS OF MINING SITES

In terms of wildlife conservation interest, mining sites can be divided into three broad groups, reflecting the categories of mining with the greatest impact:

1. **Deep-mine sites:** These include abandoned collieries comprising derelict buildings, roads, yards, building rubble, rail trackways etc., stocking areas, spoil-heaps, tail washing lagoons and small water features.

2. **Opencast sites:** These include land restored to agriculture or amenity, aquatic and terrestrial habitats, after opencasting operations but not land being mined.

3. **Subsidence wetlands:** These include surface land that has subsided due to deep-mine activities, and has subsequently become inundated.

A further distinction may also be made by dividing post-industrial mining sites into (a) those subject to restoration (i.e. with human intervention towards a designed outcome) and (b) those that are naturally regenerated (where natural processes predominate).

Along with these it is worth noting that the impact of coal mining can also include the wider or more localised hydrological and pollution impacts described earlier. Both deep-mining and opencast can have or may have had major air pollution and atmospheric fall-out effects over a wider hinterland. Similarly, associated coking or other works have had devastating effects on the region's environment (for example Orgreave near Sheffield), and Coalite in North Derbyshire. Furthermore, many industrial sites are not simple. They often have several centuries of varying modes of extraction and processing to give a palimpsest of industrial landscapes. These may culminate in massive, large-scale opencast extraction and restoration. These are dynamic landscapes in the truest sense!

COAL MINING AND ITS WASTE TIPS: A SHORT HISTORY

THE EARLIEST MINES AND TIPS, AND THE DEMAND FOR FUEL

The legacy of the coal mining industry in the form of colliery waste tips is widespread throughout South Yorkshire. The tips vary considerably in both size and age. Many of the smaller ones are earlier in origin and often are the result of both coal mining and ironstone mining. The larger tips are entirely the products of nineteenth and twentieth century coaling operations. (Similar but discrete sites such as Tinsley Park, before opencasting, was the result of metal processing over coal wastes).

No tips are known from the very earliest mining operations despite archaeological records of coal associated with Romano-British kilns at Cantley, near Doncaster (Lewis, 1971). There are no records of coal mining or utilisation in the *Domesday Book* of 1086, and no substantiated evidence until the thirteenth century. In 1287, it was recorded that a man was killed in a pit near Birstall, West Yorkshire (*op. cit*).

Mining development accelerated slightly following the signing of the *Magna Carta* in 1215. This gave landowners the opportunity to exploit minerals, including coal, and to trade in them. Thus by the end of the reign of Edward I (1307), there was small-scale coal mining associated with an increase

Table 1. Changes in fuelwood prices 1451-1642

Date	1451-1500	1531-40	1551-60	1583-92	1603-12	1613-22	1623-32	1633-42
General price of commodities	100	105	132	198	251	257	282	291
Price of firewood	100	94	163	277	366	457	677	780

[After Nef, 1966]

in demand for coal from artisans such as smiths, lime-burners, and later both brewers and dyers. The use in households created a smoke pollution problem that was the subject of a Royal Proclamation in 1306 (Galloway, 1969). This increased demand for coal coincided with a significant decrease in the amount of fuelwood available and its rising cost (Table 1); placing a severe strain on the ability to heat and cook in cities such as London.

Some compensation for the problems in domestic burning of coal was made through the design of chimneys and fireplaces and eased the associated pollution in London during the fourteenth century. It also encouraged increased output, mainly from sea coal and from mines in north-east England.

Industrial demand for fuel was rising and so some expansion in production was noted during the fifteenth century. Along with this was the sinking of newer mines especially in the northeast and in west Yorkshire.

THE TECHNICAL PROBLEMS OF THE EMERGING INDUSTRY

Expansion in the development of mining activities in South Yorkshire was somewhat later than in the Tyne and Wear valleys. This was due in part to the lack of navigable rivers and other forms of transportation. However, by the sixteenth century (between 1550 and 1615) it was recorded that there were collieries at Ardsley, Barnsley, Brampton-en-le Morthen, Greasbrough, Rotherham, Silkstone, Thurnscoe, Wales and Woodsetts (Nef, 1966). It is recorded that in 1580 a colliery with eight employees at Sheffield Park produced 1,316 tons of coal for local consumption (Lewis, 1971). The coal was being produced from the shallower seams and was mined via 'bell-pits' in such a way as to create large lumps, thus reducing the amount of waste from small coal for which there was no ready market. Any lump coal was simply stockpiled at the colliery until it could be taken away. Small coal was either burned locally or was confined to the waste along with other 'dirt' lithologies such as shale, mudstone and sandstone.

In trying to reach coals at deeper levels mining was beset with problems including water and the build up of gases such as methane and carbon dioxide. In the early, shallow mines drainage was effected by digging 'soughs' to allow the water to flow from the mine under gravity. Fires were set at the bottom of shafts to encourage an updraft and thereby a simple ventilation system. Even so, the problems of poor drainage, limited depth and poor ventilation, limited the distance worked from the base of the shaft. This situation persisted through most of the seventeenth century. Output in some areas improved through the building of wooden railways that could carry the coals from the mine to the staithes on the local river for export.

The dawning of the eighteenth century saw major progress in engineering with the development of steam power, the smelting and casting of iron, and the application of these materials and technologies to mining problems. A Newcomen pump engine which could raise water from 50-60 fathoms [91.5-109.8m] was installed in Yorkshire in 1714. This meant that shafts could be dug wider and deeper, to 150 fathoms [274.5m]. Due to this advantage from two Newcomen engines in 1739, the number increased to twenty-six by 1775. The Earl Fitzwilliam for example, had a Newcomen engine installed at Elsecar colliery in 1812, to remove 748,800 gallons per day so that he could sink a deeper shaft (Lewis, 1971).

Ventilation problems were tackled by the introduction of gateways to allow for the 'coursing of the air' around the coal-faces before reaching the up-cast shaft. In 1769, a fan, driven by a steam engine was first used to increase the rate of removal of foul air from the mine. However, this did not totally overcome the problems of mine gases. It was left to the invention and use of the Davy lamp in 1816, to identify the potential hazards of gas, and improvements to ventilation techniques such as the increasing use of electric motors for the driving of fans, that occurred by the end of the nineteenth century.

Transport both below and above ground was improved by the introduction, in 1776, of wooden tubs with iron wheels running on iron rails, a feature which was introduced in Sheffield by John Curr working for the Duke of Norfolk and widely adopted in the Yorkshire Coalfield. However, the production from the South Yorkshire area was still limited to the local market - supplying the iron and cutlery industries and local households. It was the Acts of Parliament of 1733 and 1751 to allow work to be undertaken to make the River Don navigable, and followed by the construction of the local canals i.e. the Barnsley, and the Dearne and Dove that permitted greater export of coal from South Yorkshire.

Increased demand and better transport encouraged the establishment of new collieries and the sinking of shafts through the overlying younger sediments of the 'concealed' coalfield to seams at greater depths. It was during the nineteenth century that shafts penetrated through the Permian sediments and down to the thicker Barnsley, Silkstone and Parkgate seams. In 1838, the Barnsley seam was reached in the Oaks Colliery, at 262m, and by 1866 the Barnsley seam was reached both at 382m at Denaby, and further east at Cadeby at a depth of 715m (Church, 1986).

The Victorian period saw many advances in technology coming together to increase the rate of mine development. New major surface railways with increasing numbers of steam locomotives both increased consumption of coal and facilitated effective transport. Coal use increased from 2m ton in 1869, to 12m ton by 1900 (Lewis, *op. cit*). This was the golden age of coal mining in South Yorkshire such that by 1913 output reached 287m tons per year. Pumping was becoming more efficient, and so too were ventilation and gas control. They were in part controlled through the change over from 'pillar and stall' working to 'advancing long-wall working' in panels, the dominant method of winning coal by the 1900s.

NATIONALISATION

During the early part of the twentieth century, expansion was limited by the lack of ability or willingness of the coal owners to invest sufficiently to increase productivity. The problem was in part due to the mineral rights being scattered amongst landowners and mine owners each with limited investment potential. Along with this and a serious deterrent to investment were the high risks involved. In 1938, the *Coal Act* was passed by Parliament to abolish private ownership of coal deposits and coal royalties. These passed to the state. During the early to mid twentieth century production was disrupted by the two great wars, yet the industry was still attempting to produce more coal from deeper mines, to the east, as the shallower mines, in the west, became exhausted. One of the last shafts to be sunk during this period was at Dinnington in 1925. There was some change in mining methods with a greater adoption of long-wall working, but the industry was beset with transport limitations underground (i.e. ponies), and short sections before corners and drifts were encountered.

The period from the 1930s to the end of World War Two, saw some increase in output primarily by increasing the workforce. Even so, the efficiency of such systems was very limited because faces were migrating away from the pit bottom. For example, by 1943, out of 615 collieries, with 250 men underground, some 407 were working faces over 2,000 yards [1,829m] away from the shaft with no man-riding facilities. Time at the coal face per shift was therefore very limited. Ponies were being replaced by rope haulage that occupied some 25% of the underground workforce, and therefore were non-productive (Ashworth, 1986). Conveyor systems were known about but were not widely adopted.

This scenario led to a major debate by the *Technical Advisory Committee*, and ultimately led to the publication of the *Reid Report*. This identified the disparate nature of the industry, the small-scale operations and therefore the limit on major investments. Major reorganisation and rationalisation was required but the response by the coal owners was slow e.g. of 125 separate collieries only twenty-two had plans for refurbishment or new shafts or new drifts. Of these, only two were in progress in 1945; all others being scheduled for some time after 1950 (Ashworth, *op. cit.*). As coal rights and royalties were under the direction of the *Coal Commission* from 1942 it was not surprising that Parliament passed the *Coal Industry Nationalisation Act* in July of 1946, and brought the National Coal Board (NCB) into being on January 1st, 1947. The NCB set about the re-organisation and rationalisation by setting out its strategy in '*The Plan for Coal*' published in 1950. This was based primarily upon a reconstruction of existing collieries rather than a plan for totally new ones. The plan outlined developments including twenty-two major new large collieries, sixty-seven major reconstructions, 192 minor reconstructions, with fifty-three drift mines and between 350 and 400 small collieries to 'disappear' either through closure or through amalgamation with neighbouring pits (Ashworth, *op. cit.*). Sadly by 1955, only twenty-two schemes had been completed. However, closures, largely through exhaustion, were beginning to happen e.g. twenty-one in 1947 (including Brierley) and thirty-five in 1948.

By this time the East Pennine Coalfield (Yorkshire, Derbyshire and Nottinghamshire) was the leading producer in the UK. As the geological conditions were a little less complex than in some of the other fields, it saw a major period of investment and innovation into mechanical techniques of winning coal, improved transport systems, ventilation, winding and coal preparation. With all these improvements the output per man was still not rising fast enough. It was taking three shifts to recover one stint of coal:

- **Shift 1** to cut under the coal and shotfire;
- **Shift 2** to load the coal on to the conveyors; and
- **Shift 3** to reset the props and the conveyor for the next shift 1.

Improvements in coal cutters, shearers and then shearer loaders coupled with improvements in conveyors did bring about improvement in output for the many longwall faces now being operated. In Yorkshire, the last two collieries to be developed were at Kellingley, near Featherstone in 1958 and the revolutionary concept of a mining development for the Selby Mines. Between 1976 and 1981 ten shafts were sunk and two drifts constructed for the Selby mine. Ventilation, men and materials entered the mine via the shafts, whilst the coal was transported to the surface via a belt conveyor. This terminated at Gascoigne Wood. At the same time in 1980, a new 8.0m shaft was sunk at Maltby to improve the winding capacity of the mine.

MEANWHILE BACK AT THE TIP

The waste tips produced by the industry were influenced by several factors combined. These included:

1. Changes in demand for a quality product for specific markets;

2. Increased numbers of shafts being sunk; and

3. The development of new roadways to reach new reserves.

The changes in demand saw a transfer from **large lump coal**, to the sale of **small coal** to industry. This change necessitated the introduction of screens as early as 1760, so that the different grades of product could be obtained. Indeed, even the small coals were screened a second time to separate the 'nuts' from the 'duff' that was then sent off to the tip. By the nineteenth century mechanical devices for inverting tubs – *'kick-ups'* or *'tumblers'* – had been introduced which tipped the coal onto screens where teams of young men and boys hand-picked stone, shale and 'brass' (Iron Pyrite) as the coal was moved along. Further mechanisation saw the introduction of *'jigging screens'* and then on to washing (in the 1880s), allowing coal to be separated from other sediments according to their specific gravities (based on coal being lighter). Further development of the separation techniques followed from the 1940's where, for example 35% of coal was cleaned by hand in 1947, until 1971 when hand picking ceased. This left all coal to be mechanically cleaned (Ashworth, *op. cit*). The principal reason for this change was due to the change in the nature of the coal product being produced by the new machines.

Without markets, much of the fine coal was sent to the tip until it was found that Power Stations could use it in fluidised bed furnaces. However, such a high proportion of fines had to be reduced, so coal washing was improved with increased throughputs. For example, the washer at the Manvers Colliery, the largest in the coalfield, could wash 1,340 tons per hour. Enhancement followed with the introduction of 'froth flotation' that permitted a further separation of the fine coal from the 'ash'. This left the ash to be disposed of at the tip. Computer control of the whole process reduced the ash going to the tip to 2% of throughput by 1982.

Techniques in shaft sinking, from working with hand tools to working with mechanical picks, drilling machines and the use of blasting, meant that much of the stone and mud-rock was extracted in larger lumps and transferred from the shaft directly to the tip. In many cases, the shaft waste forms or formed a smaller, discrete tip alongside which a larger tip has developed from the mining wastes. In the twentieth century, the reconditioning and reconstructing of shafts added fresh

Table 2. Changes in the coal product.

	1947	1962	1978
Dirt	10%	30%	40%
Coal > 100mm	31%	13%	8%
Coal < 25mm	40%	67%	80%

rock material to the tips along with the coal wastes. Similarly the driving of new headings to give access to new faces at different levels also produced considerable amounts of rock material that was added to the tips.

RE-SHAPING THE TIPS

The construction of the tips varied from place to place. The early ones were built up by tipping material from the tubs alongside a railway giving a long, low elongate profile. Aerial ropeways and buckets could move more material but they created conical tips, the sides of which were at angles reflecting the angle of repose of the grade of material i.e. about $30°$ to $35°$. Combinations of cones created elongate but equally steep sided tips. The determining influence on pit tip shape and form changed dramatically in the late 1960s. Following the Aberfan disaster in 1966, new laws were passed by Parliament based on the advice of the **Mines Inspectorate**. These changes included:

1967 The Mines and Quarries (Notification of Dangerous Occurrences) (Amendment) Order

1968 The Mines and Quarries (Tips) Act

1971 The Mines and Quarries (Tips) Regulations

1972 The Mines and Quarries (Tipping Plans) Rules

The net result of all the legislative changes was that tips were re-graded to reduce slope angles and to make sure that no tip would slide down slope.

Slurry lagoons were constructed to take the waste from the washeries, and to allow the fine material to dry out and become congealed. Thus the majority of the larger tips, many started in the nineteenth century and added to during the twentieth century had their form changed very markedly. Many of the smaller ones were left untouched. This clearly had a huge impact on the emerging ecology of many of these sites; often reverting the successional processes back to the beginning.

There is one problem with tips and their drainage that still remains somewhat intractable. This is 'acidity' and 'acid minewater'. This problem stems from the fact that during the time of the formation of the Coal Measures, in their swampy environment, bacteria were actively creating iron pyrite from the decomposing vegetation of the day. Some of this pyrite was mobilised to create larger, brassy yellow nodules both within the coal seams and also in the associated mud-rocks above and below the seam. However, the greater amount was as fine framboidal structures disseminated throughout the coal and the associated mudrocks. *In-situ*, below ground, the pyrite is inert. However, as soon as it is released through the mining process it begins to oxidise, changing rapidly into much more troublesome by-products such as iron sulphate, [a food substrate for certain bacteria], and sulphuric acid. This is the source of the high acidity levels in the coal waste and one that only reduces very slowly through weathering. Due to this extreme environmental factor, many of the pioneer plants appearing on waste tips are tolerant of low pH values. Their activity over time helps to ameliorate the extreme conditions.

The water draining from the tip provides a suitable habitat for both iron and sulphur bacteria. These in due course turn the sulphates into oxides and hydroxides, leaving a bright orange deposit of ochre on the stream-bed and sides of the channels. In some other cases it is the dissolution of salts in the mud-rocks that causes the waters to become saline, and so attract a completely different and distinctive flora and fauna to the coaling or post-coaling site.

It is this collection of diverse landforms that has slowly been re-colonised by plants, and subsequently by insects, amphibians and reptiles, birds and other mammals. The tips have become havens for plants plus their attendant insects, birds and mammals while the freshwater lagoons or *ings* are the domain of many insects, amphibians, and birds, and the brackish water areas provide the unique habitat for halophytic flora and fauna. This great conservation interest of the former coaling sites is the subject of the rest of this paper.

HABITAT-TYPES

A wide range of habitat-types both naturally developed and 'created' can be found on mining sites. These include pioneer vegetation, grassland, swamp, open water communities, heath, woodland and scrub.

PLANT COMMUNITIES

A very wide range of the plant communities classified by the National Vegetation Classification (Rodwell, 1991 *et seq.*) can be found. Whilst most correspond to communities already described by the NVC, post-industrial deep-mining sites also support a range of unusual pioneer and early succession types (Table 3) and subsidence wetlands a range of wetland communities (Table 4).

Two pioneer communities not described by the NVC present a particularly significant feature of post-industrial deep-mine sites which have regenerated naturally. The *Agrostis stolonifera- Holcus lanatus* community is by and large species-poor and comprises common and wide-ranging species, plus a number of locally uncommon species e.g. *Dactylorhiza purpurella*, *Poa compressa* and can be very extensive as the predominant colonising vegetation on colliery spoil tips. The community is naturally developed and has a varied character ranging from fragmentary colonising vegetation on bare ground (which can account for over 80% samples) to almost complete cover in which the grass *Agrostis stolonifera* predominates.

Agrostis stolonifera and *Holcus lanatus* are constant although the latter characteristically only occurs at low cover. Other grasses never achieve the frequency or cover of the two constants, but *Poa pratensis* and *Agrostis capillaris* can be frequent, the latter prevalent in more closed stands. Of note is the almost complete absence of grasses that are generally common in the surrounding landscape, and are more typical of 'unimproved' or partly 'improved' grasslands such as *Festuca rubra*, *F. ovina*, *Trisetum flavescens*, *Briza media*, *Alopecurus pratensis* and *Phleum pratense*. Grasses typical of improved agricultural grasslands such as *Lolium perenne* and *Dactylis glomerata* are also virtually absent. A large range of small herbs is associated with the community, almost all at very low frequency, but only *Hypochoeris radicata* and *Tussilago farfara* achieve constancy in some stands and these are assigned to different sub-communities. There can, however, be an apparent patchy dominance of some species such as *Reseda luteola*, *Hypericum perforatum* and *Elytrigia repens* on particular sites where their tall and prominent growth stands out against the bare ground.

SUB-COMMUNITIES

Agrostis stolonifera sub-community

This is the typical sub-community and has the two constants but a very variable set of associates. In some stands, particular associates can be visually prominent, either throughout as with the tall *Reseda luteola* or in patches such as with the grass *Elytrigia repens*.

Invasion by birches *Betula pendula* and *B. pubescens* and by other trees and shrubs such as *Quercus petraea* and

Table 3. Plant communities on deep-mine sites, Yorkshire Coalfield.

Agrostis stolonifera-Holcus lanatus pioneer vegetation No NVC equivalent
Vulpia bromoides-Arenaria serpyllifolia pioneer vegetation
U1 *Festuca ovina-Agrostis capillaris-Rumex acetosella* grassland
U2 *Deschampsia flexuosa* grassland
H9 *Calluna vulgaris-Deschampsia flexuosa* heath
MG1 *Arrhenatherum elatius* grassland
MG7 *Lolium perenne* grassland
MG9 *Holcus lanatus-Deschampsia cespitosa* grassland
MG10 *Holcus lanatus-Juncus effusus* rush pasture
MG12 *Festuca arundinacea* coarse grassland
CG 3d *Bromus erectus* grassland
Anthyllis vulneraria lawns
Festuca rubra-Lotus corniculatus grassland
S12 *Typha latifolia* swamp
S19 *Eleocharis palustris* swamp
W10 *Quercus-Pteridium aquilinum-Rubus fruticosus* woodland
W16 *Quercus spp.-Betula spp.-Deschampsia flexuosa* woodland
Calamagrostis epipejos sample
Plantation scrub/woodland

Table 4. Plant communities at subsidence wetlands, Yorkshire coalfield

S4 *Phragmites australis* swamp
S5 *Glyceria maxima* swamp
S12 *Typha latifolia* swamp
S14 *Sparganium erectum* swamp
S15 *Acorus calamus* swamp
S19 *Eleocharis palustris* swamp
S28 *Phalaris arundinacea* tall-herb fen
MG9 *Holcus lanatus-Deschampsia cespitosa* grassland
MG10 *Holcus lanatus Juncus effusus* rush pasture
MG6 *Lolium perenne-Cynosurus cristatus* pasture
A5 *Ceratophyllum demersum* aquatic community
A11 *Potamogeton pectinatus-Myriophyllum spicatum* aquatic community
A9 *Potamogeton natans* aquatic community
A10 *Polygonum amphibium* aquatic community
W1 *Salix cinerea-Galium palustre* woodland

Salix cinerea can give a scrubby look to some stands and an indication of successional trends. A long list of open ground species reflecting the very open nature of the sub-community and the adaptability of urban, agricultural and coastal pioneers such as *Senecio squalidus* and *S. viscosus*, *Poa annua* and *Polygonum aviculare*, *Anagallis arvensis* and *Bromus hordeaceus hordeaceus*, and *Spergularia rubra* and *Arenaria serpyllifolia* is distinctive in a broad sense. As with the other sub-communities, some unusual species can be present such as the Red Data Book *Corrigiola litoralis* (Perring & Farrell, 1983), and the locally scarce *Poa compressa* (Lavin & Wilmore, 1994).

Associates can be restricted to one or a handful of sites, but can sometimes be frequent and can give the vegetation a distinct look, as with large stands of vegetation sprinkled with *Oenothera glazoviana* or *Reseda luteola*.

Tussilago farfara sub-community

Here, *Tussilago farfara* also occurs as a constant and can appear to dominate the vegetation with its large leaves in summer (Plate 4). The grass *Deschampsia cespitosa* is preferential and can be abundant but few of the other associates achieve distinctive prominence. The introduced moss *Campylopus introflexus* and *Hieracium sabaudum* group can be frequent in some stands.

Hypochoeris radicata sub-community

In this case, *Hypochoeris radicata* also occurs as a constant in a grassier and more closed sward but whilst never dominating the vegetation can appear prominent either through its rosettes or flowers. *Agrostis capillaris* is preferential and can be more abundant than *A. stolonifera*, as also is a suite of species characteristic of mesotrophic grasslands such as *Trifolium pratense, T. repens* and *Medicago lupulina*. Also preferential is the striking *Centaurium erythraea*, which along with a group of associates such as *Linum catharticum, Anthyllis vulneraria, Crepis capillaris, Carex flacca, Geranium molle* and *Vulpia bromoides* reflects the more species-rich nature of this vegetation (Plate 5).

Vulpia bromoides-Arenaria serpyllifolia sub-community

The *Vulpia bromoides-Arenaria serpyllifolia* community is of conservation significance as it is diverse and rare in the general landscape, and supports a range of ephemeral and diminutive species only found in these harsh environments e.g. *Chaenorhinum minus, Filago vulgaris, Vulpia* spp. This naturally developed community has a distinctive and readily identifiable character in which the annual grass *Vulpia bromoides* dominates in a low and sparse sward on 20-80% open ground. *Vulpia bromoides* is constant and no other species reaches this frequency, although in some stands, patches of other species such as *Sedum acre, Vulpia myuros* and *Lotus corniculatus* achieve local prominence and can give the vegetation a rich and colourful look (Plate 7). Indeed, 'islands' or patches of vegetation dominated by *Sedum acre* growing on weathered concrete spoil can appear dramatic.

Of greater significance is the presence of a range of diminutive annuals or ephemerals growing in the sparse sward, the most frequent and diagnostic being *Arenaria serpyllifolia*, but often accompanied with species more typically associated with coastal or inland sand dunes and thin, parched soils such as *Sagina apetala apetala, Spergularia rubra, Erodium cicutarium, Myosotis discolor, Anthyllis vulneraria* and *Ononis repens*. Other grasses are infrequent, but a wide range of species can occur with no clear pattern. *Holcus lanatus* is the most frequent grass, but typically with low cover. Species more typical of mesotrophic grasslands or even woodlands such as *Dactylis glomerata* and *Holcus mollis* can occur with equal regularity to those of walls, screes and open ground such as *Aira praecox, A. caryophyllea* and the locally rare *Catapodium rigidum*.

In addition to the few species occurring at low frequency, a feature of this community is the very wide range of species that occurs casually at very low frequency and cover. This includes many species typical of waste ground such as *Reseda luteola, Cirsium arvense, Plantago major, Senecio* spp., but also includes a range of other therophytes and annuals such as *Erophila verna, Cerastium glomeratum,* and *Rumex acetosella*. Indeed, an even wider range of species is certain with further sampling, and other similar species noted in the community (but not in the samples) included *Cerastium semidecandrum, Sedum album* and *Filago vulgaris*.

The *Vulpia bromoides* pioneer community typically occurs on abandoned colliery sites in areas where mixing of substrates has occurred. It is not present on the raw material freshly dumped from the mine workings themselves - the shales, sandstones and seat-earths, but occurs where other wastes, particularly processed materials such as cinders, finings, coke or slag have been dumped or mixed with the raw wastes.

PLANTS

A remarkable diversity of plant species can be found on these post-industrial sites including many locally rare and scarce as well as *Red Data Book (RDB)* and *Nationally Scarce Species (NSS)*. Again, the majority are found on naturally regenerated sites as opposed to restored sites. Other species are *Locally Scarce (LS)* Examples include:

RDB

Corrigiola litoralis

NSS

Potamogeton trichoides

Pyrola rotundifolia ssp.*rotundifolia*

LS

Juncus gerardii

Orobanche minor

Silene uniflora

VERTEBRATE FAUNA

Data on vertebrates can be difficult to assess because comprehensive, comparative data are rarely available, especially for wide-ranging species (those that require large home ranges) and for cryptic taxa which are hard to survey (NCC, 1989). Such reliable data can be collated only for a few groups where regular monitoring and recording takes place e.g. bat roosts, amphibian and reptile breeding assemblages, wintering wildfowl, and where the national status of species is known.

For the core study sites forming the background to this paper, data for mammals suggest that these areas can provide suitable conditions for a small range of species. On deep-mine sites, of most conservation significance is the regularity of sites with Brown Hare - a species where the national population trend is downwards (Harris *et al.*, 1995) and which is on the UK BAP list. The presence of 'naturally' developed habitat-types and plant communities suited to hare on some sites is probably helpful to some aspects of the species' life cycle. Sites supporting Badgers are also of significance, as this species is legally protected and in the study area is both uncommon and under threat. This species favours a mosaic of habitats (Harris *et al.*, 1995), to which these types of sites must contribute. Water Voles are also of current conservation concern as populations are declining. This is thought to be due to habitat deterioration and increased predation of depleted populations by Mink (*Mustela vison*) (Woodroffe, 1994), and the species has also been included on the UK BAP short list. The presence of this species on at least one deep-mine site contributes to that site's significance. The records of Otter (*Lutra lutra*) at two subsidence wetlands are of note given the recent recovery of populations of this species (also on the UK BAP short list) in England. In Yorkshire it is still rare with extant populations only on some of the North Yorkshire catchments (S. Jay, pers. comm.), and these records constitute examples of a tenuous range expansion (Jefferies, 1996). However, their presence indicates suitable conditions and must contribute to those sites' assessments. Harvest mice are also locally uncommon and the presence of populations is of note. In some parts of the study area they have been found to be more widespread than hitherto realised, e.g. Sheffield (Whiteley, 1996; Rotherham, 1994).

Small populations of herptiles were recorded at a number of sites. The outstanding nature conservation discovery of the study is probably the colliery pond supporting five species of amphibian in substantial numbers. One site scored highly on standard conservation assessment criteria and supports one of the best UK populations of Great Crested Newt as well as an outstanding assemblage (NCC, 1989). This site has since been proposed as a European Special Area of Conservation on the basis of the series of records obtained during the course of this study (A. Gent, pers. comm.). As Great Crested Newts are of conservation concern and are included in the UK BAP short list as well a being legally protected, the other deep-mine site supporting a small population is also of conservation significance. Whilst all herptiles are afforded some limited legal protection (*Wildlife and Countryside Act*, 1981), populations of Common Frog, Common Toad and Smooth Newt are generally widespread. Only significant populations are considered of value in formal conservation assessments. However, Palmate Newt is locally uncommon and the most rare species nationally (Swan and Oldham, 1993; Arnold, 1995). Reptiles are also difficult to assess, but are sufficiently uncommon for their presence to contribute to a site's overall value if they are found.

Although fish were not systematically recorded, and the modification of populations makes conservation assessments difficult except for very rare species (Maitland and Campbell, 1992). Some species of no interest to anglers can be of local conservation interest. In the study sites, the presence of Ten-spined Sticklebacks at two subsidence wetlands is of note, as this species is uncommon in the region (Bunting *et al.*, 1974). A summary of the key mammal, amphibian and reptiles, and fish species of conservation value on mining sites is given in Table 5.

BIRDS

The most significant bird conservation feature of mining sites is the numbers of wintering wildfowl occurring on some of the subsidence wetlands and opencast restorations. Some 16,744 waterfowl occurred at peak periods during the study period at nineteen sites, with seven individual sites each supporting over 1000 waterfowl and in total around 81% of this population (WeBS counts, winters 1992/93-1994/95, via British Trust for Ornithology). Of these waterfowl populations, a number of species occurred in nationally significant numbers (>1% of the national population) at individual sites, notably Gadwall at Fairburn Ings and Swillington, and Shoveler at Fairburn (Table 6).

For nine species, Yorkshire subsidence wetlands and restored opencast wetlands support significant proportions of the GB wintering populations - Little grebe 2.4%, Whooper Swan 1.2%, Gadwall 4%, Shoveler 3.9%, Tufted Duck 3.4%, Pochard 2.0%, Goldeneye 1.1%, Goosander 1.2% and Coot 3.7%. Populations at individual sites supporting between 0.1% and 0.99% of the national population could be regarded as regionally significant, for example at the West Yorkshire level (A. Barker, pers. comm.), and certainly those sites supporting a number of species within these thresholds could be regarded as more significant than others. However, some of the data must be treated with some caution, since some of the species concerned e.g. Little Grebe, are widely dispersed on other water-bodies. These not counted under the national scheme and therefore the national populations are likely to be underestimated. Nevertheless, the data support the contention that wintering waterfowl populations at these sites, and particularly the top seven, are of substantial conservation interest.

Further bird conservation interest is apparent from breeding populations, especially of the subsidence wetlands. Using the standard criteria for SSSI evaluation for breeding bird assemblages (NCC, 1984), two sites are of particular significance for bird assemblages - Broomhill and Fairburn

Table 5. Conservation assessment of mammals, herptiles and fish found on study sites.

Species	Conservation Criteria	Assessment
Brown Hare	UK BAP short list	presence contributes to site value
Badger	Badger Act	presence contributes to site value
Otter	UK BAP short list W & CA (1981)	presence contributes to site value
Water Vole	UK BAP short list	presence contributes to site value
Harvest Mouse	locally significant	presence contributes to site value
Great Crested Newt	UK BAP short list W & CA (1981)	sites are important in own right
Palmate Newt	locally significant	presence contributes to site value
Amphibian Assemblages		sites are important in own right
Grass Snake	locally significant	presence contributes to site value
Ten-spined Stickleback	locally significant	presence contributes to site value

Ings, with a diversity of species, some in significant and regular numbers, notably of waterfowl. Whilst the evaluation is targeted towards the selection of SSSIs at national level, it is also clear that other wetlands have breeding bird communities bordering on such status e.g. Edderthorpe, where recognition at regional level would be appropriate. Some caution needs to be taken with the data, since 5-year data sets ideally need to be used in this sort of analysis, and the figures are derived from data in local bird reports for the years 1991-1995, where some years' data are missing. Nevertheless, data from the two key sites for the years 1996-1997 reinforce the evaluation (D. Waddington pers. comm., *Fairburn Ings Bird Reports*).

In addition to the national and regional significance for waterfowl and breeding bird assemblages for open waters and their margins, all types of site have some bird significance at local level. Waterfowl sites supporting hundreds of birds are clearly of local significance, whilst some of the species in the breeding bird assemblage are also localised because of the restricted habitat availability. In addition, deep-mine sites can also be of some significance for some species.

Table 6. Significant wildfowl sites in the study region.

Site	Species														
	Lg	G	C	M	W	Ga	T	Wi	M	Sv	Tu	Po	Gy	Gs	Co
Fairburn	0.5	0.	0.5	0.6	0.8	1.7	0.3		0.2	1.5	0.7		0.4	0.6	0.9
Anglers		0.			0.2		0.1			0.5	0.7	0.4	0.2	0.3
Pugneys	0.2	0.		0.2			0.1			0.6	0.6	0.2	0.1		0.3
Rother Valley											0.2	0.3			0.3
St Aidans	0.1		0.2			0.2				0.1	0.8	0.5	0.2	0.2	
Broomhill	0.1			0.3			0.2		0.1	0.3					0.1
Swillington	0.2			0.1	1.1					0.8	0.2			0.2	0.1
Mickleton	0.7			0.1		0.3					0.1				0.2
Denaby Ings	0.1									0.1					0.2
Catcliffe											0.1	0.1			0.2
Sprotboro	0.2									0.3					0.5
Allerton	0.2										0.1				0.1
Altofts										0.2	0.1	0.2			0.5
Stanley	0.1														
Total	2.4	0.	0.7	0.9	1.2	3.5	0.6	0.1	0.3	3.9	3.4	2.0	1.1	1.2	3.7

National percentages of wintering wildfowl at subsidence wetlands and restored opencast sites

In bird conservation terms the most important feature of deep-mine sites could be argued as those supporting Little Ringed Plovers since the total national population estimate for this species is around 600 pairs (Parrinder, 1989), and the twenty-one pairs at eleven of the forty-six deep-mine sites represents 3.5% of the British population. In addition, six wetland sites also supported the species with an estimated population here of six-ten pairs, giving a total of twenty-seven –thirty-one pairs or 4.5-5.2% of the national population on the seventy core study sites. Some caution needs to be made to the figures, since some of the wetlands were adjacent to the deep-mine sites and birds may have been double counted. However, many other deep-mine sites in the Yorkshire coalfield were not sampled in the study, and it is likely that the total population of this species in the study area will be higher. Opencast sites can also hold exceptional numbers of this bird. The Killamarsh Meadows opencast (now Rother Valley Country Park), in the 1970s, held up to eighteen pairs.

The significance of other deep-mine site species can, on the one hand, be viewed as being local, in that assemblages of scrub and grassland birds occur on the more well-established sites, and contribute to local biodiversity. On the other hand, many once-common species have recently declined e.g. Tree Sparrow (*Passer montanus*), Corn Bunting (*Miliaria calandra*) (Marchant et al., 1990), and some of these have been included in the national lists of conservation priorities (Gibbons *et al.*, 1996; UK Biodiversity Action Plan, 2002) If these species occur significantly on mining sites, they may be assumed to be contributing to biodiversity conservation at a national level.

This analysis outlined in Table 6 suggests that deep-mine sites are of conservation value for Grey Partridge, Quail, Skylark as breeding sites and foraging areas for broods, presumably because of good insect populations not affected by pesticides; for roosting Reed Buntings, Corn Buntings, Starlings, Swallows and Sand Martins in reedbeds; as foraging areas for Green Woodpeckers (found regularly on sites); for foraging Kestrels; and breeding Grasshopper Warblers. On subsidence wetlands and opencast wetland restorations for wintering wildfowl (six species), breeding Garganey, Snipe, Curlew, Shelduck and Redshank; roosting Starling, Sand Martin, Swallow; breeding Reed Bunting, Kingfisher and Grasshopper Warbler; foraging Kestrels and wintering Lapwings and Golden Plovers. The analysis reinforces the important features derived from other methods, although the significance of the breeding Little Ringed Plover population is not highlighted in this analysis.

INVERTEBRATES

Given the limited quality of the data on invertebrates of these sites, the conservation value of the core study sites cannot be systematically addressed. Only general inferences can be made and these should be considered in the context of work done elsewhere (e.g. Eyre & Luff, 1995). There are one or two exceptions to this. The significance for some sites for butterflies lies with the large populations of more common species that contribute to the intrinsic appeal of sites, as well as to the reservoirs of local populations. Some species e.g. Common Blue can be rare in some areas e.g. Calderdale, West Yorkshire and therefore their presence, especially in quantity contributes to sites' overall assessment. However, few sites are regularly counted for numbers although this situation is changing with data published for 1996 including large counts at some of the study sites of 163 Small Skippers, and 840 Gatekeepers at Fairburn Ings, and 379 Common Blues, 150 Gatekeepers and 134 Meadow Browns at Walton Colliery. The most significant butterfly found (at four deep-mine sites, one in significant numbers) was Dingy Skipper, a local species thought to be declining. Its food plant, *Lotus corniculatus* was abundant on some sites. (This species was also found at one of the other derelict mine sites, Holbrook in Sheffield. Here it is locally very rare). Marbled White, a regionally scarce butterfly was also found on one site. Further research revealed that it had been introduced and therefore of limited value in a conservation assessment.

For Odonata, sites supporting breeding assemblages can be compared for assessment. Threshold numbers of species being of value in different regions of the UK. Data are however rapidly increasing, and with a new range of observers and recently produced field guides, meaningful assessments may be problematic. At the time of writing effective criteria had not yet been revised, particularly where the assemblage contains widespread species. Of the taxa recorded from the study sites, at the time of the surveys *Lestes sponsa, Libellula quadrimaculata, L. depressa, Sympetrum sanguineum, S .danae, Aeshna mixta*, and *A. cyanea* can be indicative of conservation value as they are locally scarce. Based on this, two deep-mine sites (Gipsy Marsh and the reclaimed Walton Colliery) stand out. In recent years however, the Odonata generally have expanded in range and abundance at many sites.

The highly unusual brackish invertebrate interest at the subsidence wetland of Mickletown Ings is of significant scientific interest, and can contribute to the site's conservation interest on the criterion of rarity.

The most significant invertebrate data from the study is apparent from Coldwell's data at the deep-mine sites of Manvers, Falthwaite and Cortonwood colliery tips, although with Crossley there were interesting records from Thorne Colliery. Using standard assessment methods the Manvers site scores 1,740 with numerous RDB and Notable species. The threshold figure for consideration as a SSSI is 200 and whilst any assessment of a site needs to be treated with some caution to take account of the intensive recording by a specialist, it is still clear that this is an outstanding site for insects, and clearly demonstrates the value of open ground environments. Combined assessments for three sites with data are given in Table 7.

EARTH SCIENCE FEATURES

No sites proposed for *Regionally Important Geological Sites* (RIGS) status were identified in the Jeff Lunn study. However, it is recognised that certain colliery tips can prove to be valuable for geological aspects of nature conservation. At Wath Main colliery tip, examples of molluscan fossils were found in small, scattered locations on top of the colliery spoil tip, but not in any great concentration. Ian Rotherham and Tim Wootton found abundant specimens of fossil ferns from the Coal Measures in excavated material at the Waverley opencast coal site south of Sheffield in the 1990s. Almost all was subsequently lost to a combination of weathering and land shaping. An Internationally Important site, recognised as a "stratotype section" of the Mansfield Marine Band, demonstrates features of this marine incursion as well as being the international boundary between the Westphalian B and C divisions of the Carboniferous Coal Measures, is interpreted at the site which is located in a part of the brickworks quarry at Stairfoot. A second site, recognised as a regional geological SSSI, is the outcrop of the Top Marine Band located in part of the Carlton brickworks quarry at Grimethorpe. Clearly opencast sites such as the now restored Waverley mine in Rotherham for example, may also produce large amounts of major and impressive plant fossils. There seemed to be little interest shown by any of the authorities in the rescue and presentation of any of these. In consequence they are now well and truly restored!

Table 7. Invertebrate evaluation from three deep-mine sites, Yorkshire.

Species Status	Score (Ball, 1986)	Manvers	Cortonwood	Falthwaite
RDB1	100	1		1
RDB2	100	2	1	
RDB3	100	2	1	1
pRDB1	50	1		
pRDB3	50	1	1	1
Nb	40	7		
Nr (NE)	20	24	1	
Notable	40	7	2	
Notable g)	20	5		
TOTAL		1740	350	250

NATURE CONSERVATION EVALUATION

The data suggest that great wildlife interest can exist on land affected by mining and using established methods (Ratcliffe, 1977), these can prove to have value for nature conservation. Admittedly, features of international or national importance are rare, though not unknown. Of more significance is the regularity and frequency of features significant at a regional and local level e.g. some pioneer environments and communities, birds and invertebrates. The data from naturally regenerated sites clearly reveal a wide range of nature conservation interest including plant and animal communities and species, and earth science features. A summary of the key features is given in Table 8. Significance is demonstrated from the European level to local level for different attributes. However, as a general guide, deep-mine sites are of value for open ground and early colonisation features (whether terrestrial or aquatic), and opencast terrestrial sites for heath and grassland derived from natural regeneration. Wet opencast and subsidence sites have significant potential for wetland plants and animals.

In contrast, the restored, terrestrial, deep-mine sites hold negligible value for wildlife. Some of the restorations of tips to grassland support the BAP species Skylark, and young plantations hold local breeding bird communities. However, a very significant contrast exists between these sites and the much richer naturally regenerated sites. The range and quality of significant features is much less on the restored sites. Opencast sites restored to agriculture have virtually no interest.

Whilst this is the case for deep-mine terrestrial sites, wetland restorations - either opencast or the deep-mine - also hold considerable nature conservation significance, particularly for aquatic and swamp communities and birds. Similarly, subsidence wetlands hold considerable interest, although a difference exists between the two categories, with the opencast sites being more restricted in terms of significant associated features. This is to be expected since the opencast sites will be immature ecosystems. Also, many of the subsidence wetlands will be more likely to be near to existing wetlands, from which colonisation and expansion can take place.

In addition to the assessments of significance for flora, fauna and earth science features above, it is also apparent that many sites are close to human settlements and to major centres of population. They therefore offer opportunities for amenity, recreation and conservation activities to people in local communities - the broader elements of nature conservation. These are often in socio-economically and environmentally disadvantaged situations. The contraction of the coal mining industry in the late 1980s and early 1990s has left pit villages with high levels of unemployment and poor facilities. However, many sites offer opportunities for informal recreation such as walking, and some have more formal leisure activities programmed e.g. boating on the restored wetlands such as at Rother Valley Country Park. In recent years these opportunities have been increasingly recognised and restorations have taken them into account.

Other features are also of value in the overall assessment of sites. None of the deep-mine sites in the study had been recognised for any local history significance. When asked their views, local people did remark that following restoration it would be impossible for future generations to understand the impact of mines and the associated spoil heaps on the local landscape. It was suggested that some features could be retained (P. Middleton pers. comm. re Grimethorpe). One deep-mine restoration had symbolised the finished landscape by the placing of sculpture e.g. 'Standing stones' at Tinsley Park, or half a winding gear wheel at Upton. Similar features of half a winding wheel plus stainless steel plaques of plans and sections of strata at Wath Colliery have been incorporated into the New Wath Park. Whilst not a coaling site, but one associated with iron-stone, the potential significance of an historical landscape and environmental feature in the local area is well demonstrated by the series of 20-30 bell-pits at Tankersley (Jones, 1995). These are a most significant local history landmark, with visual impact, recorded history and current nature conservation significance. Other bell-pits at Denby Grange have also been recognised as historically significant (Hey, 1986). In this case the vegetation is much modified by agriculture.

DYNAMIC LANDSCAPE RESTORATION

In the context of the landscape of the Yorkshire coalfield as a whole, the mining industry, particularly the coal mining industry has left an extensive legacy of post-industrial land. This is juxtaposed with small settlements (pit villages) in extensive pastoral settings. During the height of production, these busy areas caused direct land loss of wildlife sites and indirect effects such as water-course pollution, noise and disturbance. Ironically, the security afforded them through their commercial lives probably had benefits for wildlife as refuges from disturbance and from the effects of agricultural pesticides and fertilisers – potentially damaging to wildlife in many semi-natural environments. More significantly these operations created a range of wetlands through subsidence. Those sites subject to natural regeneration offer unique opportunities for charting natural ecological processes such as colonisation by flora and fauna without deliberate human intervention. Unmanaged, and free from effects such as above, they have developed a wide range of wildlife features now rare in the managed and farmed landscape of the wider countryside, and some that are quite distinctive.

Survey has also demonstrated that most restorations are driven by 'greening' ideals – a hurry to cover up

Table 8: Summary of key nature conservation features of mining sites, Yorkshire.

Significance	Deep-mine	Opencast	Subsidence wetlands
International e.g. SPA, cSAC	Great Crested Newt*		
National e.g. SSSI, BAP species	Pioneer and grassland (P2, U1) plant communities

Plants - *Corrigiola litoralis**
Open ground invertebrate assemblage (Diptera., Hymenoptera)

Brown Hare*, Water Vole*
Skylark^, Grey Partridge*, Quail, Reed Bunting*, Corn Bunting*

Amphibian assemblage* | Lowland heath (H9, H8, M16) | Aquatic and swamp* plant communities

Brackish invertebrates
Swamp invertebrates

Otter*

Wintering wildfowl
Breeding bird community,
Reed Bunting* |
| Regional e.g. 2nd tier site, LNR | Pioneer and grassland communities. (P1,U2,MG1,MG9,10,12) W16 Woodland

Plants - *Oro. minor, Ophrys apifera, Apera interrupta*
Plants - assemblage of locally scarce plants

Invertebrates of open ground
Lepidoptera - Dingy Skipper, assemblages/large populations, Forester Moth*.
Dragonfly assemblage^

Great Crested Newt sites*

Bird roosts of reedbeds
Little Ringed Plover | Grassland (MG9, MG10, 'hay meadow'
Aquatic & swamp* communities
Plants - *Pyrola rotundifolia, Ulex gallii*

Wintering wildfowl
Migratory birds esp. waders
Breeding bird community
Little Ringed Plover | Aquatic & swamp* communities
Wet lowland grassland*
Plants - *Juncus gerardii, Pot. trichoides, Ran. hederaceus**

Harvest Mouse

Wintering wildfowl
Breeding bird assemblage
Migratory birds esp. waders
Little Ringed Plover*

Ten-spined Stickleback |
| Local | Badger setts

Assemblages or populations of local plants & animals^, or plant communities

Earth Science features. | | |

^ feature also found on restored deep-mine sites.
* - listed on the Biodiversity Action Plan N.B. for birds only the 'short' and 'middle' lists.

the scars of extensive and visually intrusive industry. There may also have been political expediency - to cover up the evidence and embarrassment of a collapsed industry and all that went with it. Many of the deep-mine sites have already been treated – the collieries converted to other uses such as residential or commercial parks, and the spoil-heaps smoothed into huge grassy mounds. These are much poorer in wildlife terms. On such sites where wildlife forms an integral part of the design brief within restoration (and these are very few and almost exclusively opencast restorations with a significant wetland element), the wildlife interest can be boosted considerably.

For the implementation of the *UK Biodiversity Action Plan*, itself a consequence of the Earth Summit in Rio de Janeiro in 1992, restoration of land to a 'green' after-use could be a significant contribution, especially given the extent of post-industrial mining land in the region. Advice is available to practitioners and decision-makers at levels from national to local. Indeed, the costs of incorporating such methods into an overall scheme are negligible (Rotherham & Lunn, 2000). It is therefore tragic that far more restoration schemes have not sought to pursue this line. Ironically, wildlife conservationists and local naturalists will have had only a brief period in-between the cessation of the regional mining industry and restoration, to appreciate the value and diversity of post-industrial mining sites for wildlife. Their impact on the landscape and potential environmental and cultural value has been and will be quickly swept away by 'greening' programmes and a lot of public money.

REFERENCES

Anon. (1990) *Sheffield and Rotherham City Airport – Environmental Statement*. Shepheard Epstein and Hunter, London.

Ashworth, W. and Page, M. (1986) *The history of the British Coal Industry, 1946 – 1982 : The Nationalised Industry*. Volume 5. Clarendon, Oxford.

Atkinson, F. (1968) *The Great Northern Coalfield, 1700 – 1900*. University Tutorial Press, London.

Beynon, H., Cox, A. and Hudson, R. (2000) *Digging Up Trouble- The Environment, Protest and Opencast Coal Mining*. Rivers Oram Press, London.

Bownes, J.S., Riley, T.H., Rotherham, I.D. and Vincent, S.M. (1991) *Sheffield Nature Conservation Strategy*, Sheffield City Council, Sheffield.

Church, R. (1986) *The History of the British Coal Industry, 1830 – 1913: Victorian Pre-eminence*. Volume 3. Clarendon, Oxford.

Eyre, M.D. and Luff, M.L. (1995) Coleoptera on Post-industrial Land: a Conservation Problem? *Land Contamination and Reclamation*, **3(2)**, 132-134.

Galloway, R.L. (1969) *A History of Coal Mining in Great Britain*. Reprint of the 1882 edition. David and Charles.

Hatcher, J. (1993) *A History of the British Coal Industry before 1700: Towards the Age of Coal*. Volume 1. Clarendon, Oxford.

Lewis, B. J. (1971) *Coal Mining in the Eighteenth and Nineteenth Centuries*. Longman, London.

Lunn, J. and Wild, M. (1995) The Wildlife Interest of Abandoned Collieries and Spoil Heaps in Yorkshire. *Land Contamination and Reclamation*, **3(2)**, 135-137.

Middleton, P. (2000) The wildlife significance of a former colliery site in Yorkshire. *British Wildlife*, **11**, 333-339.

Nef, J.U. (1966) T*he Rise of the British Coal Industry*. Volume 1. Cass & co., London

Rotherham, I.D. (1999) Urban Environmental History: the importance of relict communities in urban biodiversity conservation. *Journal of Practical Ecology and Conservation*, **3(1)**, 3-22.

Rotherham, I. D., Cartwright, G. and Watts, R. (2000) *Airport, Steelworks or Historic Landscape – the Sheffield Airport development as a case study of integrated site planning*. SER 2000 Conference, Liverpool (Abstract paper).

Rotherham, I.D. and Boon, G. (1988) *A Preliminary Assessment of the Ecological Value of Tinsley Park (SK 405 884); and Geology of Tinsley Park Area*. Natural Sciences Section, City Museum, Sheffield.

Rotherham, I. D. and Lunn, J. (2000) *Positive restoration in a 'Green Belt' open-cast coaling site: the conservation and community benefits of a sympathetic scheme in Barnsley, South Yorkshire*. SER 2000 Conference, Liverpool (Abstract paper).

Watts, R., Pearson, R. and Rotherham, I.D. (1987) New Life for the Lower Don Valley. *Landscape Design*, **165**, 16-19.

Wild, M. and Gilbert, O.L. (1988) *Sheffield Inner City Habitat Survey*. Sheffield City Wildlife Group, Sheffield.